# SATURDAY
# NIGHT
## AT THE
# MOVIES

CLASSIC *f*M

# SATURDAY NIGHT
# AT THE
# MOVIES

The extraordinary partnerships
behind cinema's greatest scores

JENNIFER NELSON

First published 2018 by
Elliott and Thompson Limited
27 John Street
London WC1N 2BX
www.eandtbooks.com

ISBN: 978-1-78396-366-9

*Picture credits:*
Page 3: Cindy Ord/Stringer/Getty Images; page 11: Steven D. Starr/Getty Images; page 23: Kevin Winter/Getty Images; page 41: AF archive/Alamy Stock Photo; page 63: ScoringSessions.com; page 81: Everett Collection Inc/Alamy Stock Photo; page 103: Jeff Vespa/Getty Images; page 123: Columbia/Kobal/ REX/Shutterstock; page 139: Kevin Winter/Getty Images; page 163: AF archive/ Alamy Stock Photo; page 183: ScoringSessions.com; page 205: Boston Globe/ Getty Images; page 221: Barry King/Getty Images

9 8 7 6 5 4 3 2 1

A catalogue record for this book is available from the British Library.

Typesetting: Marie Doherty
Printed in the UK by TJ International Ltd

# CONTENTS

# INTRODUCTION

Picture the scene: you're in the cinema, the lights go down and you settle in, ready to be entertained, moved or challenged. A few hours to escape from everyday life and be transported to another world. The music you hear forms as much of the experience as what you see on the screen. It can take many forms – subtle and creeping or bombastic and brash – but when successful, the score is an inextricable part of the film. This book explores how some of the world's best-loved composers and directors work together to bring a film to life by fusing sound and vision.

What is the secret to successful creative collaboration? Friendship, a shared goal, being in the right place and time – or another special ingredient that's less easy to define?

Film directors often surround themselves with a core team of people they work with regularly, but there's something unique about the partnership they have with a composer. Together, the two have the potential to create a seamless dynamic between what's heard and what's seen on the screen, enhancing the audience's experience by building their emotional connection to the story.

*Saturday Night at the Movies*, Classic FM's weekly film music programme, first explored this subject in 2014 when it was hosted by the composer Howard Goodall, and it's one that current presenter Andrew Collins has returned to over the years. The collaboration between John Williams and Steven Spielberg is perhaps the most influential and impressive in cinema history: nearly thirty films together in over forty years. With an array of instantly recognisable themes ranging from ominous (*Jaws*), to heartbreaking (*Schindler's List*) and triumphant (*Raiders of the Lost Ark*), Williams has the power to get to the heart of the story. Bernard Herrmann and Alfred Hitchcock form another iconic 'power couple' thanks to their combined contribution to the art of suspense, most notably with masterpieces like *Vertigo* and *Psycho*. Yet after just over a decade of working together, they had an almighty falling-out and their collaboration came to an abrupt end. Creative partnerships don't always last forever.

As we'll see, the secret to collaborative success is not as simple as two people getting on. Ego and trust can affect the power balance – but should a film director and composer view each other as equals in the first place? Alan Silvestri describes Robert Zemeckis as 'the captain of the ship', which suggests a deference to the vision of the director, but he also compares their long-standing collaboration to a marriage, in which each party respects and supports the other. Generally, it is perceived that the composer (as with all other crew members) should answer to the director, but, as Howard Goodall points out, 'It's also true to say that a lot of the directors in this book acknowledge the fact that the music can completely change the mood and the impact of a film. They acknowledge how important the composer's input can be – that's not always the case – and how it can lift the film from being quite a good film into something with a huge impact, through brilliant use of music, or a brilliant idea in the orchestration, or a brilliant way of looking at it.'

A great film composer writes music that envelops the audience, immersing them more deeply in the story unfolding on-screen. For a director to be aware of that power is one thing but for them to trust another individual to provide the musical reflection of their vision is another, especially as most successful directors are, by their own admission, control freaks. Are disagreements to be encouraged? Conflict can be a healthy part of collaboration, ensuring each delivers their most effective work, but in intense, high-pressure environments like film sets personalities can clash badly. What's significant is whether, and how, the director and composer choose to patch things up, from Michael Giacchino and J.J. Abrams getting things out in the open with an 'honesty pact' to James Cameron and James Horner allowing themselves breathing space after the production of *Aliens* before working together a decade later on *Titanic*, to monumental success. Even Christopher Nolan and Hans Zimmer, who describe themselves as close as brothers, admit to fighting like cats and dogs, and the director accepts that he pushed the composer to his limits when scoring *Dunkirk*.

The twelve partnerships featured here are some of the most creative in the business. Some have worked together for years; others have made a significant impact with a select number of films. But they are all responsible for some of the best-loved scores in the world. It hasn't escaped our attention that this is not the most diverse list, but it does seem that steps are being taken to broaden opportunities for aspiring composers and directors from all backgrounds.

The collaborators in this book all have different ways of working but one universal exercise is the spotting session, when a rough cut of the film has been assembled and the two watch it together, discussing which scenes need music and what sort of music is required. More often than not, the film will have been put together with a temporary, or 'temp', score, a compilation of other music to give the composer a steer. This can be helpful to provide an idea of tone or style, but can also be limiting because it does not offer a blank canvas to the composer, and thus risks imitation. In the case of Peter Jackson and Howard Shore, the director used cues (tracks from specific scenes that make up a film score) from the composer's previous films to temp his initial footage of *The Lord of the Rings*. On seeing how well the visuals matched the music, Jackson invited Shore to join the team and the composer created a sound world using specific musical themes, known as leitmotifs, to represent the vast array of characters and cultures that inhabit Tolkien's universe.

Communication between the director and composer is crucial. The director needs to be able to convey their artistic objectives but while they may be fully confident of articulating their vision, it's not always easy to describe music with words. Goodall is not convinced that it helps if the director is musical: 'Most composers would say they don't care either way but they want to have responsibility for the musical choices that take place. I think if they were being undiplomatic they would say a director who really knows what they want from the movie is more important to them than a director who can say, "Can it sound a bit like Vaughan Williams or Shostakovich?" When you have the vocabulary of music, you have a vocabulary that is very full of jargon and specifics, and that doesn't always translate itself to people who come from other fields. I think it's probably more helpful for a composer that the director is very sure of the overall effect that they're trying to go for, and that the composer uses that information to turn it into their response musically.'

Whether or not a director is musically literate, they will of course be well versed in the technicalities of film-making. Goodall believes that 'one of the reasons that the relationship between composer and director has become a unique one in film history is because of the coming together of two technical worlds that they both are completely immersed in. They're not the same, but they interlock. There's no sense that they're competing with each other but they can make each other better.' That lack of competition may be important in the highly pressured world of film-making, with its fierce deadlines and equally fierce financial demands. Many composers in this book praise their directors for shielding them from these pressures and giving them the space to create – because it takes time to come up with the perfect theme to elevate a story.

Communication, mutual respect and a shared desire to get to the heart of the story are just some of the key factors that will crop up throughout this celebration of director–composer collaborations. Interviews and behind-the-scenes stories offer an insight into their working methods as well as the wider film-making process, and if reading the book is anything like writing it, prepare to feel the urge to watch or re-watch some of the finest movies ever made, from *Lawrence of Arabia* to *Titanic*, *Inception* to *E.T.*, *Skyfall* to *Back to the Future* – perhaps with a keener ear than before. There is a suggested playlist at the end of each chapter and you can find a selection of the music at classicfm.com/snatm – just in case you want to listen along to the film scores as you read!

# 1

# CARTER BURWELL AND THE COEN BROTHERS

*'Carter is never the problem.'*

There are movies and then there are Coen Brothers movies. Joel and Ethan Coen have written, directed, produced and edited seventeen films in over three decades and each one is unique, with characters, settings and plot twists that are unlikely to be found elsewhere at the cinema. This is precisely what defines their work: their films are stand-alone oddities that may be funny or gruesome or unpredictable – often all three at the same time – as they jump between genres and play with cinematic conventions. From cult favourites such as *The Big Lebowski* and *Raising Arizona* to box-office hits like *True Grit* and the Academy Award-winning *Fargo* and *No Country for Old Men*, Joel and Ethan – working so closely they have been referred to as the 'two-headed director' – make films that can entertain and baffle in equal measure. When accepting the Oscar for Best Director, Joel described their early attempts at filming with a Super 8 camera in the local shopping mall

1

when younger brother Ethan was eleven or twelve, declaring, 'Honestly, what we do now doesn't feel that much different from what we were doing then', before acknowledging their standing within the left field of Hollywood: 'We're very thankful to all of you out there for letting us continue to play in our corner of the sandbox.'

Whether comedy, film noir, western or a gangster movie, composer Carter Burwell has joined them in the sandbox for fifteen films, with T Bone Burnett taking over the music supervisor and producer roles on the folk and country-music soundtracks for *O Brother, Where Art Thou?* and *Inside Llewyn Davis*. Since getting his break on their debut feature, *Blood Simple*, in 1984, Burwell has gone on to score around a hundred films. He received his first Academy Award nomination in 2016 for Todd Haynes's *Carol*, and his second followed soon after in 2018 for *Three Billboards Outside Ebbing, Missouri* directed by Martin McDonagh.

Describing the composer, Ethan – generally the more upbeat of the two – has said, 'By Hollywood terms, he's unbelievably normal and well balanced. It's almost alarmingly normal.' Joel, with his more sombre and laconic delivery, agreed: 'He's refreshingly not a lunatic.' Ethan continued, 'We were talking about musicians and T Bone was talking about a drummer called Bill Maxwell and he said, "Bill is never the problem." You so much know what he means because everyone else always can be. Carter is never the problem.'

⌁

Carter Burwell met the Coen Brothers through another long-standing collaborator, Skip Lievsay, who has served as sound editor on all of their feature films. The brothers were preparing to make their first feature, **Blood Simple** (1984), a violent and stylish black comedy starring Frances McDormand, who would go on to appear in many more of their films

Carter Burwell (right) with sound editor Skip Lievsay
at the Tribeca Film Festival, 2015, discussing 'The Sound of the Coens'.

(and who married Joel the year the film came out). According to Joel, 'Carter at the time was not a practising movie composer, or really a music composer of any sort. He had a musical background but at the time I think he may have been, or had been, working in a science lab in Long Island, which is one of his other interests. But Skip said, "This guy could definitely do this", and of course, we were all just kids at the time! We met Carter, we went over to a loft that he had, with this big old peeling [piano] and talked about what we were doing, or what we wanted to do, and Carter went off from there.'

The composer has a slightly different recollection: 'Years later I asked Joel why they had hired me or what that process had been like ... He said he had done a lot of interviews with composers and they were looking for someone who knew what they were doing. That would not have been me at the time, I had no experience of film music and no knowledge of it!

'He said that these are still among the strangest interviews that he's ever done. They've auditioned hundreds of actors over the years but he felt that the composers were the oddest bunch, so I guess apparently out of that odd bunch I count as being normal! . . . Joel and Ethan and I see each other as having the same sensibilities, coming from a similar view of cinema and humour, so in that sense we see each other as normal. We simply have similar tastes and we'll see the same awful story and laugh at it, and that's important in their films to be able to do that.'

With simple piano motifs and electronic effects, the score for *Blood Simple* could be described as 'minimal', although Ethan is quick to clarify 'minimal by choice and by necessity 'cos there wasn't any money!' It remains one of Burwell's favourite scores, 'partly because I didn't know what I was doing, so I just ignored the entire film-making process and wrote some little pieces of music that I liked. I can't really do that any more because I'm now expected to be a film composer, but with *Blood Simple* I didn't know how it was supposed to work, and Joel and Ethan didn't really know how it was supposed to work, so there's a certain innocence that comes with that that you can't really recapture.'

❧

The Coens' roster of long-time collaborators includes cinematographers Barry Sonnenfeld and Roger Deakins, set decorator Nancy Haigh, production designer Dennis Gassner, co-editor Tricia Cooke, storyboard artist J. Todd Anderson, costume designer Mary Zophres, and Peter Kurland, who has worked in the production sound department of all of their films. With their 'hands-on' approach to film-making, it's no surprise that the brothers stick to working with people they trust, and over the decades they have built up a select group of actors who have made regular appearances in their films, such as John Turturro, John Goodman and Steve Buscemi.

Burwell, meanwhile, has formed regular partnerships with other directors. He has worked with Bill Condon on six films, including *Mr Holmes* and *Gods and Monsters*, and with Spike Jonze, Todd Haynes and Martin McDonagh on three. You could argue that the quirky style of *In Bruges* by McDonagh or Jonze's *Being John Malkovich* isn't a million miles away from Coen Brothers' fare, but Burwell has proved he can also turn his talents to mainstream blockbusters, scoring three of the five films in the teen vampire-romance franchise *Twilight*.

The Burwell–Coen partnership is the only trio collaboration within this book, and Carter notes the effect of an additional person on the dynamic: 'It does balance out the ego a little bit, the fact that there are two of them. They generally present themselves almost as being one mind, but that's easily overstated because in fact they're very individual people and I've seen the two of them disagree about the music in the films, about the role of it or what it should be doing, so it's not exactly true that they always come from one place. But by the time I'm involved, they've written the film together, and they generally have a clear understanding and agreement of what they're trying to make.'

On the balance of egos between composer and director, Burwell is typically down to earth: 'Well, I know that I'm not the best composer in the world, so it's not that difficult for me! But I certainly know film composers who have egos, so it is possible to have an ego and still be a successful film composer. For myself, I really feel I'm still learning all the time . . . and taking that point of view brings a certain humility with it.'

The Burwell–Coen relationship seems pretty secure but, even with a hit rate of fifteen out of seventeen films, they still approach collaboration on a film-by-film basis. As Joel points out, 'There's a sort of distinction that has to be made between most of the movies. Almost every one of the movies that we've made, we've made with Carter. The exceptions are that we've made a number of movies that have minimal score or no score, and are essentially driven by source music or performed music in the movie itself. With those movies we often have at least a partial idea of what the music is going to be because it's drawn from either popular music or folk music. With the stuff with Carter, it's a little different. Sometimes we know in a general feeling kind of way and sometimes we don't.'

The composer describes the general pattern of the scoring process: 'It always starts with a script. They'll give me a script sometimes well in advance of their shooting – it could be more than a year before they shoot – but if they have good reason to believe it's actually going to get shot, they'll give me a script so if nothing else we can at least talk about budgets because it helps them formulate one if we decide it's four players, or it's eighty players. But we'll also throw around ideas about what the music is going to do . . . most of the time, there's no expectation that we're really going to figure it out at the script stage, but other times the problem of the music is a big one and is something we really do throw around early on.'

Both directors and composer used **True Grit** (2010), the revisionist western adaptation of the 1968 book by Charles Portis, as an example of tackling the music early on in the film-making process. As Burwell explains, 'There had already been a film of *True Grit*, so the question was: "What are we going to do that distinguishes our film from that? What's going to be different from it?" Joel and Ethan had already made films that featured authentic country music (see *O Brother, Where Art Thou?*) and they didn't really want to do a western score or a faux western score' – or, in Joel's words, 'We didn't want twangy guitars or Ennio Morricone.'

The story of Mattie Ross, a fourteen-year-old farm girl who hires Deputy US Marshal Rooster Cogburn, played by Jeff Bridges, to track down the outlaw who killed her father, *True Grit* required a certain kind of music to set it apart from the 1969 original (with John Wayne as Cogburn), which, as Burwell acknowledges, 'had a wonderful Elmer Bernstein score', so the composer turned to the main character for inspiration. 'I had read the book, I had read the screenplay, and we got together just before they left to shoot. I said that my thought was that the book is narrated by the girl and her voice is present on every page, and you're constantly hearing references to the Bible, church, sin, judgement, and her church background sort of explains why she does what she does, but that's not so present in the movie. So I thought that one thing that would help was if the music emphasised this church background, and if we worked from hymns for the score in some way, whether it was sung or played orchestrally or on a different instrument – and Ethan said he'd been thinking about the same thing!' From Ethan's point of view, 'That's why Carter's great. He always knows it's about the characters and that's where I'm going mentally first to think about the score.'

While the brothers were shooting the film, the composer was trawling through nineteenth-century hymnals and collecting Protestant hymns, such as 'The Glory-Land Way' and 'What a Friend We Have in Jesus', to reorchestrate or reference in the final score. One highlight is 'The Wicked Flee', a simple piano tune based on the hymn 'Leaning on the Everlasting Arms', which is elevated by soaring strings in the final thirty seconds. The same infectious refrain, used as Mattie Ross's theme, features in other cues like 'Ride to Death' and 'River Crossing'. Due to the presence of pre-composed hymns, Burwell's score was deemed ineligible for the Academy Award for Best Original Score, but *True Grit* received ten nominations in total, including Best Director, Best Picture and Best Adapted Screenplay. It went home empty-handed, but remains the Coen Brothers' highest-grossing film to date.

⤗

Burwell is keen to point out that working with the Coens can be very different from working with other directors, which can be a big advantage when it comes to the score: 'It doesn't really get concrete until they show me some footage. With Joel and Ethan, unlike most directors, they're happy to show me a rough scene put together. Because we know each other so well, and because they write and produce and direct and edit their films, we all have a pretty good idea of what it's going to be. There isn't really any uncertainty, there aren't any other personalities that are going to suddenly appear and change the film. If we're talking about what we think it's going to be, that's what it's going to be.

'What I've just said might seem obvious to some people but in fact film isn't typically done that way. Probably most feature films involve a lot of unpredictable input from producers and executives, and they test the films in front of audiences and those tests can result in changes, so it's not necessarily true that once you've read the script or even once you've seen the first rough cut that you actually know what the film in the end is going to be – but with Joel and Ethan, typically you do.'

⤗

Returning to the start of their partnership and careers, the Coens followed *Blood Simple* with **Raising Arizona** (1987), a kidnapping comedy which was by all accounts a conscious decision to create something lighter and with more sympathetic characters – although a violent and unpredictable streak remains in this tale of Hi and Ed, a childless couple who steal a baby. Burwell tried out new sounds and styles, and the main title, 'Way Out There', is a gloriously bonkers musical journey, starting ominously before introducing a frenetic banjo, wistful whistling, and finally some spritely yodelling – all in under two minutes. Burwell's detailed website provides information and composer's notes about his scores, and it states that the music for *Raising Arizona* was largely 'improvised using household objects – vacuum cleaner hoses, hubcaps, peanut butter jars'.

Displaying a tendency to leap across form and genre – it's quite common for the Coens' films to alternate between light-hearted and darker tones – their next project was the neo-noir gangster film *Miller's Crossing* (1990). This was their third collaboration and the composer's first orchestral score: 'No one other than the Coen Brothers would've hired me to do an orchestral score knowing that I knew nothing about orchestral music!' It was certainly a leap from the banjo, but the large orchestra allowed for a more traditional sound to fit the Prohibition-era setting. Burwell based most of the score around Irish folk ballads to complement the story of double-crossing Irish mobsters and the stirring end titles, based on 'Lament for Limerick', provide a beautiful contrast to his earlier scores. By this stage, the composer had proved his versatility and appetite for new styles, instruments and performers, which has only continued throughout their partnership.

⸝

Their sixth collaboration, *Fargo* (1996), was the brothers' breakout film. A critical and commercial success, it won Academy Awards for Best Original Screenplay and Best Actress, for Frances McDormand, from a total of seven nominations, including Best Picture. *Fargo* premiered at the 1996 Cannes film festival and Joel won the Prix de la mise en scène, the Best Director Award – a solo winner despite the fact the brothers work as a pair, because up until *The Ladykillers* (2004), Joel was credited as director and Ethan as producer. *Fargo*'s enduring popularity is evident in the Emmy Award-winning television series of the same name, set in the same fictional universe and executive produced by the Coen Brothers.

The dark comedy crime thriller following a pregnant police chief investigating roadside homicides opens with this perfectly pitched text: 'This is a true story. The events depicted in this film took place in Minnesota in 1987. At the request of the survivors, the names have been changed. Out of respect for the dead, the rest has been told exactly as it occurred.' As you read this on the screen, you hear the gentle harp of 'Fargo, North Dakota', which leads you from the black background to a white wall of snow, gradually building until you can make out a car driving towards you. It's a simple scene of a car towing a trailer, but in Burwell's hands, complete with dramatic drums and crescendos, the tone is austere and spellbinding.

Burwell chose this, along with *Blood Simple*, as his favourite Coen Brothers' score: 'I'm certainly very proud of *Fargo* for a variety of reasons. Both the score and the film are very good and very individual. They're not really like anything else. I'm also proud because I think that was one of the first scores I orchestrated myself, and conducted, so it was a big step for me.' He based the main musical motif on a Norwegian folk song called 'The Lost Sheep', and used a traditional Scandinavian instrument, the Hardanger fiddle, to add fragility and 'a shimmering glowing drone to the played notes'. There is sadness and depth throughout – the perfect foil to the dark humour – and the elegant melancholy of 'Safe Keeping' could easily play bedfellow to Burwell's later Academy Award-nominated score for *Carol*.

Joel recalls *Fargo* as an example of the composer creating something exceptional with minimal direction: 'We didn't quite know what we

Ethan and Joel Coen at the Academy Awards in 1997,
where they won Best Screenplay for *Fargo*.

wanted and Carter came up with some sketches and then we said, "No, you know, what we really think is going to work is something that's a lot bigger and operatic and orchestral." And he went away and did that beautiful score for *Fargo*, just essentially . . . on that information. Melodically, he was inspired by some Scandinavian folk thing but that was him taking that cue and going off and doing something totally different with it.'

⁂

Part of the success of the *Fargo* score is due to its sombre tone, which enhances the film's comedic elements. On his website, Burwell refers to the challenge of scoring dramatic music that provides 'exaggerated seriousness' to complement or underplay scenes that veer deftly between laughter and surprise or shock in the audience. The Coen Brothers are fond of experimenting with light and shade in their film-making, and Burwell's scores similarly tease the audience's expectations: 'They like to work with a genre, like the western or the film noir, so we're inevitably working with the tropes of that genre. They do it when they're film-making and writing, and I'm doing it in the music too. A lot of scores to comedies are just full of parody and winks at different musical genres or different films, and we don't do much of that, but we are definitely commenting on the traditions of particular genres.'

The Coens' most recent comedy, *Hail, Caesar!* (2016), is set in the Hollywood film industry of the 1950s. A fictional tale about real-life 'fixer' Eddie Mannix, played by Josh Brolin, who spends his time keeping his actors on the straight and narrow, it gave the pair the opportunity to recreate films of the era, including a Roman epic and set pieces for synchronised swimmers and singing cowboys. This required a broad musical palette, as Joel explains: 'It does by necessity have to jump all over the place . . . the question was, how much do you have to link all of those things and how much can you move around and still have it feel as a sort of coherent score for the movie? It was a little bit delicate, but [Burwell] came up with this central theme for the biblical movie that we realised also was going to work in different orchestrations for vastly different parts of the actual movie.'

The theme is played on solo piano at the start as Eddie Mannix sits in his car on a rainy night, and reappears to rousing effect in the title cue with all the brass you could shake a *Ben-Hur*-sized stick at. It returns with woodwind and strings as Mannix sets out to find who kidnapped actor Baird Whitlock (George Clooney), with percussive flourishes and a choir providing the finishing touches to 'In Pursuit of the Future'. According to Ethan, 'The ambition was to come up with something for Josh's character that would work . . . for the Roman movie within the movie . . . Actually, our one specific point of reference was Alex North who did the score for *Spartacus*, kind of like that in terms of feeling, and that was repurposed in a more pompous way for the Roman part of the movie.'

Some of their earlier comedies relied less on score than on existing songs, with Burwell filling in the gaps, such as *The Big Lebowski* (1998).* The eclectic soundtrack features Kenny Rogers, Bob Dylan, Henry Mancini and Nina Simone, and Burwell provided some original cues including the techno-pop homage 'Wie Glauben', a million miles away from his usual sound-world.

On other occasions, Burwell has had to compose around existing classical music, most notably Beethoven piano sonatas in *The Man Who Wasn't There* (2001). The brothers had written the music into the script, and as Ethan explained, 'That was an interesting discussion because we were thinking... "What's going to sit well with the Beethoven?" and we agreed quickly that Carter was not going to compose some faux Beethoven. Carter came up with something which is totally a different idiom but really just the thing.' The closing piece, 'The Trial of Ed Crane', is aching and delicate, and Ethan seems to find these cues particularly arresting, referring to Burwell's work on the comedy drama *A Serious Man* (2009): 'Just very spare piano, which is really beautiful. I don't quite know how to connect it in a literal way with the movie but it's just the thing for that movie.'

The composer used percussion to connect to the scheming, incompetent characters in the black comedy *Burn After Reading* (2008), most notably in 'Earth Zoom (In)' and 'Night Running', which he explains was an early concept: 'They liked it right away. And the idea that because the characters all imagine themselves to be at the centre of some international

---

* The 1998 tale of mistaken identity, bowling and, yes, kidnap again, was not a commercial success but has since garnered such a wide fanbase that there's an annual festival in its honour and a religion, Dudeism, based on the philosophy and lifestyle of the lead character, Jeffrey Lebowski.

intrigue when in fact they're not, using that as a jumping-off point for the music, that feels logical. But actually finding the right tone for George Clooney and his part of the story, how dark should it be or how musical or how spy-like – that took a little bit of time to figure out.'

≈

Music is scarce in ***No Country for Old Men*** (2007), the Coen Brothers' award-winning adaptation of the Cormac McCarthy novel, but when it appears during the end credits, you certainly know it's there. Considered by many to be Joel and Ethan's masterpiece, this cat-and-mouse thriller set in the desert landscape of west Texas has been described as a 'neo-western' and 'neo-noir', packed with memorably tense scenes featuring Javier Bardem as Anton Chigurh, one of the greatest on-screen villains of recent decades. Bardem won the Academy Award for Best Supporting Actor, and the Coens picked up the Oscar for Best Director, Best Adapted Screenplay and Best Picture.

Burwell estimates that there is probably only about thirteen minutes' worth of score throughout the entire film. You might not even notice any music at all: 'It is hidden always. Sometimes you hear it disappear but you never hear it appear, and it's always blended into things like the sounds of tyres on a pavement or the wind, because every time when we would watch it, every time we would be aware that there was music, it would lower the reality level of the film and the stress would go out of it in some way. The silence in the film, the quietness, is the thing that really put you on edge.'

He still thinks of new ideas for what might have worked for the score even now. 'Blood Trails', which played over the end credits, was initially written to feature in the film itself, but the directors were keen to avoid a typical score. They later recalled their initial discussions with Burwell about the film's musical direction, acknowledging the score as 'probably one of the strangest assignments Carter's ever had'. They wanted music for the end credits, but couldn't give him any kind of brief or context for what they were after. In Joel's words, 'It could be anything, and probably nothing will work!' Somehow Burwell came up with the goods, as Joel described it: 'It was so smart: he'd listened to the last scene and he took the music out of that ticking clock, which was kind of the beat in the kitchen there, and it was . . . perfect.'

For his part, the composer saw 'Blood Trails' as a good way to segue viewers gently and seamlessly from the film's silence to a piece of music. 'It begins in this very minimalist way, with just a shaker. Skip [Lievsay] and I arranged a sound design and a segue into the score, so that the sound of the film ends on a ticking clock and that brings you into the shaker of the end credits, then slowly works through some of the ambient sounds that I used in the film that don't even sound musical, and then eventually a guitar appears.'

⁓

The success of the Burwell–Coen partnership is due partly to a shared sense of what works and what doesn't, but Burwell knows from experience that this isn't always the case: 'Any collaboration is political. I have my ideas of what the music will be, which is not always going to be the same as the director. Hopefully we see the big picture the same way, and disagree about some of the smaller things. Some directors will just say, "No, that's not going to work, do something different." Joel and Ethan will usually give me a lot of rope with which to hang myself.' He points out that he knows the Coens well enough to be able to sense from their tone of voice whether or not they feel he's on the right track. For their part, the Coens point to Burwell's versatility as a huge asset.

According to Ethan, 'Carter will do almost anything. Musically he's a real chameleon, as you have to be if you're scoring movies' – especially Coen Brothers movies.

Burwell describes their working relationship as 'really not like work at all because each of the three of us is simply trying to make the best movie from our point of view'. He says neither he nor the Coens focus on thinking about how the film might be received by an audience or the studio or anyone else, which not only makes the process easier but enables them to be bolder in what they set out to do: 'It means you can take more chances because I don't have to worry that someone's going to come back and say, "What in the world are you thinking?" As long as the three of us see the logic of it, and see that this is the best way to go, then the job is done.'

When asked for his advice to aspiring film composers, Burwell places communication at the heart of collaborative success: 'Every director is different, so you just have to be sensitive to that, as a composer. I like to always have some concept behind the score, if only for myself, and I'm usually prepared to verbalise that so when I play it . . . I can explain it, which isn't always easy to do with music.' Ultimately though, for him, it's the score you write that matters: 'You have to watch the film with the music and feel that it's doing the right thing, it's making the film better, it's saying something that isn't otherwise there, creating a richer experience . . . No amount of reason or concept is going to be more important than that.'

## Collaboration History

(All films directed, written, produced and edited by Joel and Ethan Coen)

*Blood Simple* (1984)

*Raising Arizona* (1987)

*Miller's Crossing* (1990)

*Barton Fink* (1991)

*The Hudsucker Proxy* (1994), co-written with Sam Raimi

*Fargo* (1996)

*The Big Lebowski* (1998)

*O Brother, Where Art Thou?* (2000)

*The Man Who Wasn't There* (2001)

*Intolerable Cruelty* (2003), co-written with Matthew Stone and
    Robert Ramsay

*The Ladykillers* (2004)

*No Country for Old Men* (2007)

*Burn After Reading* (2008)

*A Serious Man* (2009)

*True Grit* (2010)

*Hail, Caesar!* (2016)

 ## *Suggested Playlist*

*Raising Arizona*, Way Out There (Main Title)

*Miller's Crossing*, End Titles

*Fargo*, Fargo, North Dakota

*Fargo*, Safe Keeping

*The Big Lebowski*, Wie Glauben

*The Man Who Wasn't There*, The Trial of Ed Crane

*Intolerable Cruelty*, Intolerable Mambo

*No Country for Old Men*, Blood Trails

*Burn After Reading*, Night Running

*A Serious Man*, A Serious Man

*A Serious Man*, The Roof
*True Grit*, The Wicked Flee
*True Grit*, Ride to Death
*Hail, Caesar!*, 5 a.m.
*Hail, Caesar!*, Hail, Caesar!

# 2

# PATRICK DOYLE AND
# KENNETH BRANAGH

*'You save an awful lot of time when you're
ahead of someone's thoughts.'*

Spanning Shakespeare and superheroes, Patrick Doyle and Kenneth Branagh have worked together on twelve films, from *Henry V* in 1989 to *Murder on the Orient Express* in 2017. While adaptations of the Bard's works might seem to dominate the list, the variety of musical styles and film genres covered – the romantic *Cinderella* (2015), the unsettling *Sleuth* (2007) and the action-packed *Jack Ryan: Shadow Recruit* (2014) – remind us that this is a versatile partnership, as well as a successful one.

Their success can be attributed to talent, of course, but also to a firm and loyal friendship that has strengthened over the decades. As Doyle has said, 'We get on terribly well. He's a very funny person, very witty. He's one of the smartest people I've ever met and has a great instinct for music and drama. He allows me to have lots of artistic leeway but the whole experience is hugely enjoyable. We have an instinctive rapport, there's a symbiosis there which either you have with a director or you don't.'

Their collaboration stands apart from others in this book because the director may actually be better known to many for his acting work on stage and screen. Branagh's directing skills are just a part of his varied career and he is the first person to have received Academy Award nominations in five different categories: Best Director (*Henry V*), Best Actor (*Henry V*), Best Live Action Short Film (*Swan Song*), Best Adapted Screenplay (*Hamlet*) and Best Supporting Actor (*My Week with Marilyn*). Meanwhile, Doyle has had cameo roles in seven of Branagh's films, so both have experience in front of the camera as well as behind the scenes.

The director has an eye and an ear for a good story, which Doyle acknowledges: 'I've been very fortunate that his choices have been very astute, very classy.' Still, as he explains, 'every film's difficult ... You've got to deliver the best work you possibly can, and it has to be of a very high standard. I put my heart and soul into it. But there's no special dispensation for a pal.'

⤳

Belfast-born Kenneth Branagh attended the Royal Academy of Dramatic Art and, at twenty-three years old, was the youngest ever actor to play Henry V in a Royal Shakespeare Company production. He co-founded the Renaissance Theatre Company with David Parfitt in 1987, and their third production, after *Romeo and Juliet* and a one-man show with John Sessions called *Life of Napoleon*, was a staging of *Twelfth Night* at Riverside Studios in Hammersmith, featuring an original score by the actor, composer and musician Patrick Doyle.

Doyle, from South Lanarkshire, had studied piano and singing at the Royal Scottish Academy of Music and Drama, and after meeting

Kenneth and joining the team for *Twelfth Night*, they hit the road: 'We did a national tour with Judi Dench, Derek Jacobi and Geraldine McEwan directing. Three plays: *As You Like It*, *Hamlet* and *Much Ado About Nothing*. I was employed as a musical director. I played small parts in it, but really my job was as composer and music director. As it was a rep company, the fact I could do a bit of acting was all to the good! At the end of that tour, the Renaissance Film Company was then established, and I went on to do *Henry V*.'

The tour not only established long-lasting partnerships between Branagh and the other actors – he directed Dench and Jacobi as recently as 2017 in *Murder on the Orient Express* – but also laid the foundations for a solid working relationship between him and Doyle. 'He certainly became aware of my musical facility for melody,' recalled the composer. 'The fact that I could work fast also really appealed to him. So that helped to cement our relationship.' Doyle has spoken in interviews about the significance he places on the narrative and characters within the films he scores, and his early career as an actor may have influenced this approach. He watches film rushes with an acute eye, looking to ascertain whether music is required to elevate a scene or an actor's portrayal. The composer's preparation involves spending some time with the cast, which is vital for Branagh: 'He knows that performances are so key to me, that he wants to get a sense of who they are and how they speak about their characters.'

⁓

*Henry V*, their first feature film collaboration, was also Doyle's first movie and he had a small role as Court, a soldier in Henry's army. He is the first to start singing the film's stand-out piece of music, 'Non Nobis, Domine', during a long, sweeping shot as the camera follows Branagh carrying the body of Robin, played by a young Christian Bale, through the battlefield. It's a significant moment in the film and for Doyle's career as a composer: he won the Ivor Novello Award for Best Film Theme.

The composer has cited *Henry V* as an example of how Branagh briefs him and communicates his creative objectives at the start of a project, recalling how the song came into being, nearly thirty years ago, as they sat in the dressing room of the Palace Theatre in Manchester: 'He described this shot in detail, and that the music should build and build. His reference was – and this may seem odd – the Paul McCartney Frog Song ['We All Stand Together'] . . . I thought of 'Tomorrow Belongs to Me' from *Cabaret*, that's the way I saw it in my head, with that kind of growth in a musical track. So I went into the foyer of the theatre, and I wrote the tune. It took five minutes! I immediately wrote another tune because I thought, "That came out too quickly", but . . . usually your first idea's the strongest one. I went back to him after lunch and played it to him and he says, "The first one, that's it, definitely." And this piece has been my calling card for the rest of my film career!'

Branagh's *Henry V* won universal acclaim for bringing his theatrical flair to the silver screen, and made the actor and director a household name. Still considered one of cinema's finest Shakespeare adaptations, it received three Academy Award nominations, including Best Actor and Best Director, and won the Oscar for Best Costume Design.

For his next project, Branagh chose to direct a markedly different film, the Hitchcockian romantic neo-noir **Dead Again** (1991), in which he and his then-wife Emma Thompson played the lead roles. Doyle provided an appropriately thrilling and tense score, with stand-out cue 'The Headlines' serving up a bold concoction of strings, woodwind with sudden brass flourishes; he received a Golden Globe nomination for his work.

Patrick Doyle and Kenneth Branagh at the premiere
of *Cinderella* in Los Angeles, 2015.

❧

When asked about his composing methods, Doyle says, 'I move fairly
fast', although he is more measured these days, allowing himself some
time to digest the script and consider the film before starting to compose.
'I tended to be more impatient when I was younger,' he reflects, and
credits those vital early discussions with Branagh for providing initial
inspiration.

Being on location has its uses too, as was the case for their next collaboration, *Much Ado About Nothing* (1993), one of the most financially
successful Shakespeare adaptations of all time. Branagh turned the witty
play into a hugely entertaining film with a great cast including Denzel
Washington and Michael Keaton. Doyle plays Balthazar, Don Pedro's

musician, and performed some of his own songs including 'Sigh No More, Ladies'. He spent six weeks on the set in Tuscany, which had a big influence on his subsequent score: 'Strangely enough, the overture was written on the banks of the lake of Menteith, the only lake in Scotland, but all the inspiration was from my work in Italy.'

The pair are on the same page when it comes to the secrets of their collaborative success, as Branagh has said: 'Because Pat and I are very good friends, have known each other a long time now, when I know that a movie may be on the horizon, I let him know very early on and he's always keen to have an initial conversation, just to have a sense.' Sometimes this can take place as far as eighteen months ahead of any recording stage, allowing ideas to settle and take shape in Doyle's mind early on: 'That's the way we work together: the earlier the better, and then you become really embedded in the film with the director.'

⁓

Their next Shakespearian adaptation was the first unabridged screen version of *Hamlet* (1996). At over four hours it's a lavish and ambitious visual feast, expertly carried by a superb cast including Julie Christie, Derek Jacobi, Kate Winslet and Branagh himself in the lead role. *Hamlet* received four Academy Award nominations, including Best Original Score for Patrick Doyle, his second nod after *Sense and Sensibility* the previous year.

Again, early conversations between the director and composer were crucial for the score: 'I listen very closely to [Branagh's] first impressions of what he wants, or his first instructions as to what he wants to achieve in the picture. If you listen very closely and read the script, then that in itself conjures up musical ideas.' Speaking to *Soundtrack! The Collector's Quarterly* in 1997, Doyle revealed that while he tended to work with a temp track of his own music to avoid the age-old problem of temp scores leading to imitation, he and Branagh had agreed for this project that whenever the composer watched footage, there should be no music to steer or influence him.

The director requested a strong main theme to portray the lead character, and Doyle composed three themes in total, for the characters of Ophelia, Claudius and Hamlet. He was inspired early on to include some chamber pieces: 'The only device I thought I would use throughout the film is a quartet or a quintet that would suddenly be joined by the full orchestra . . . and then be left in isolation again and then joined.'

The scoring of the famous 'To be or not to be' scene was left until later, while they pondered whether or not it required music: 'Apart from one cutaway it's a long stationary shot. The music is there to make it more accessible to the audience and to keep the focus. I was trying to capture the essence of the scene, which deals with life and death itself and the age-old question of why we are here. I tried to give this feeling of antiquity, by having a chronological device of bringing in ancient instruments joined by modern instruments.' The result is deliberately understated, adding tension to the hall of mirrors as the Prince of Denmark contemplates suicide, watched on the other side of the glass by his stepfather and uncle, Claudius.

The two Shakespeare films that followed were adventurous adaptations, in particular *Love's Labour's Lost* (2000) – the first time it had been made into a feature film. One of Shakespeare's lesser-known comedies, it was a risky decision to turn it into an all-singing, all-dancing Hollywood musical. Unfortunately the risk did not pay off, as neither audiences nor critics could muster up much enthusiasm. Most of the music comes courtesy of early twentieth-century American composers including Cole Porter, Jerome Kern and George Gershwin, and it was

Branagh's idea to incorporate their songs within the body of the story. Doyle's challenge was to compose an underscore that fitted neatly around the familiar numbers like 'The Way You Look Tonight' and 'I Get a Kick Out of You'. His contributions have a characteristic vigour, such as 'Victory' with its triumphant brass, not dissimilar to his popular score for *Harry Potter and the Goblet of Fire* several years later.

*As You Like It* (2006) was a less daring proposition, despite also being relatively unfamiliar. This time the director chose to transport the drama to a late nineteenth-century colony in Japan. The location gave Doyle the opportunity to incorporate some Eastern sounds, including a Japanese stringed instrument called a koto, and the resulting score is superb. 'Violin Romance' is simply beautiful, and feels instantly familiar from the opening notes, whether or not you've seen the film. Doyle had another cameo role, performing his composition 'Under the Greenwood Tree', which beguiles the melancholy Jacques, played by Kevin Kline. In 2007, shortly after the release of the film, Doyle described the shoot: 'It was quite a daunting first day. You arrive, you meet the actors, some of them for the first time, like Kevin Kline, and you immediately have to teach them this song on location. I then had to teach the entire staff of Wakehurst Place [in West Sussex, where most of the filming took place] the song . . . that's the way it works with Ken, it's like "shooting from the hip", as they say, so it's always great.'

Doyle smiles at the idea that any one of the Shakespeare adaptations might have been any easier than any other: 'They're all difficult! It doesn't matter if it's your good friend or it's a director who you've never met before, you're still required to compose the score. The fact that you may have a laugh together doesn't preclude the serious work of actually delivering and coming up with the goods. Each film I do is difficult, and certainly not any less difficult working with Kenneth Branagh, especially

working on a Shakespeare adaptation. I always feel a tremendous deference towards Shakespeare because he's such a genius.'

~≈~

The romance of *As You Like It* was stripped away for their next project,
**Sleuth** (2007), a reinvention of the 1972 stage play in which two men
spar for a woman's love using tricks and mind games. Starring Michael
Caine and Jude Law, this is a claustrophobic cat-and-mouse tale, and
Doyle's score is sparse and fascinating, a world away from his Shakespeare
works. He has spoken in interviews about *Gesamtkunstwerk*, which
translates as 'total work of art', and how all elements of the film-making
process combine to complete the final product. This belief that each part
of the process is as important as any other adds to his knack for getting
under the skin of a narrative. He believes that the job of the composer 'is
to be another character and to weave yourself in and out of the drama,
as another actor appearing on the screen would be'. On *Sleuth*, his subtle
drums, elegant strings and chilling piano motif conjure an atmosphere
of calculated distance as the drama unfolds.

Another bold choice came next: the announcement that Branagh
would be entering the comic-book world of superheroes to direct **Thor**
(2011) was a surprise to many. The fourth film in the Marvel cinematic
universe, this was Branagh's return to big-budget directing after the disappointment of *Love's Labour's Lost*, and while his involvement raised
a few eyebrows, all's well that ends well because it was a well-received
critical and financial success.

The scale of the project required some adjustment for Doyle, but he
felt his relationship with Branagh was strong enough to enable him to
get some honest feedback from the director: 'It was a challenging score
because he and I were dealing with a huge franchise, and the production

executives are much more involved in every single aspect of the process of film-making, so you can lose your direction because you're dealing with a body of people, not just with the director . . . I remember calling him as a friend, not as a director, to say, "Look, I'm not sure, am I going in the right direction?" Looking back, it was just the pressure of the job. These action movies are enormous pressure for everyone, because they've got a huge worldwide exposure and lots of money invested in them. He was very reassuring . . . and a couple of days later, it was as if the call never took place.

'That's when you can rely on your friend, and be honest and say, "I'm not quite sure what's going on here in my head." You're much more on your own when you're dealing with these big massive productions because the director's got so much more responsibility in other areas . . . it's almost every man for himself!'

Doyle composed an intelligent score for a superhero blockbuster, opting for light and shade instead of an assault of crashing crescendos. He shows he's capable of large-scale majesty with 'Thor Kills the Destroyer' and offers heroism without the bombast in cues like 'Chasing the Storm'. Making musical distinctions between Earth and Asgard, he used more contemporary sounds involving electronics and percussion for the former, while Thor's realm was depicted by broader orchestral strokes. The love story between the eponymous hero and the Earth-dwelling Jane Foster is handled sensitively, and Doyle really gets the strings to sing in 'Can You See Jane?'

Following *Thor*, Doyle scored other big-budget films including *Rise of the Planet of the Apes* and *Brave*, continuing to experiment with styles and broaden his palette. The Celtic influences of *Brave*, in particular, are a welcome reminder of his diverse skill set, complemented by earlier period pieces like *Gosford Park*. As with the other composers in this book, he has benefited from working with different directors in between projects with his main collaborator, including Brian De Palma (*Carlito's Way*), Ang Lee (*Sense and Sensibility*), Alfonso Cuarón (*Great Expectations*), Robert Altman (*Gosford Park*) and Amma Asante (*A United Kingdom*). He puts this impressive roster down to personality: 'I think I have the good fortune of being a bit of a chameleon. I like to connect with people and the essential thing is to listen very carefully and try to pick up all the signals of people's artistic tastes. I think if your antenna is receptive to these things, you're halfway there.'

Loyalty is another key factor in most successful collaborations, and Doyle clearly considers it to be a fundamental requirement. In terms of his relationship to the wider production and musical teams, Doyle is firm on where his loyalties lie: 'My allegiance is always to the director. If there are any artistic differences or perceptions, then they have to deal with that amongst themselves; I deal with the director. It's the most sensible way to work. That way, you're only dealing with one person, and that person is the conduit with other people. Not all directors are obviously musical in the same way as you are, but they usually have a strong sense of what music does to their picture, and you have to instil confidence in them in your work. So you have to be quite bold and diplomatic.'

⊷

Branagh's highest-grossing film to date is the Disney live-action remake of *Cinderella* (2015), and once again he sat down with Patrick Doyle well in advance to discuss the music, although this time there was a more practical necessity to do so: 'When there are considerations like the requirement of music for the waltz that features in the film, we would need playback on set when shooting, so he's writing a tune and an arrangement maybe six months before he would normally do so; that's quite a big commitment in advance to what a central theme of the movie might be. That early collaboration is key.'

Branagh's skill of honouring the story and the characters was particularly useful for Doyle in getting to the heart of the score: 'There was no frivolous dismissal of "it's only a fairy tale". He recognised that this is one of the greatest stories ever told. He described the dilemmas that Ella had – the dysfunctional family, the multiple deaths, the darkness that's in that picture . . . I then let those thoughts process through my head for four, five days, and I sat down at my piano one day and I just played the entire opening of the principal waltz. There was no difference in Ken's mind between the characters in *Cinderella* and the characters in *Hamlet*, for example. They were just as important . . . and the same commitment and depth was required of the score.' The composer neatly avoids over-sentimentality, with music that is as magical and charming as the Disney tale requires, but never cloying.

Next came another familiar tale, albeit of a very different nature, with the fourth screen adaptation of Agatha Christie's much-loved classic mystery ***Murder on the Orient Express*** (2017). Branagh assembled another stellar cast, with Penelope Cruz, Johnny Depp, Michelle Pfeiffer, Daisy Ridley and Willem Dafoe alongside his old chums Derek Jacobi and Judi Dench, and he took on the challenge of playing private detective Hercule Poirot. The production team recreated a 22-tonne locomotive on a moving set, enabling the actors to feel that they were really on board the famous Orient Express, complete with thousands of LED screens on the windows showing passing Alpine scenery. The composer, as usual, visited the set several times, but his thematic ideas had formed even earlier, after detailed discussions about the characters with Branagh. He also saw some early footage and read the script before getting down to work. 'I presented material very early on, way back in Christmas 2016, and said, "Is that the world you expect?" and he said, "Well, it sounds like you're going in the right direction." With that, content he was on track, Doyle continued.

~

One of the most impressive elements of the Doyle–Branagh collaboration is the way they have balanced friendship with a professional partnership over the decades, defying the old adage about mixing business with pleasure. In some interviews, Doyle attributes their success and longevity to their ability to have fun: 'As soon as he starts to talk fervently about a subject, whatever it is, I just jump on board immediately. But I think what's essential to the connection is a great sense of humour.' In others, he places value on the support he receives from the director during the pressured film-making process: 'The bottom line is you have to come up with a very good score, but you're aided and abetted by a very generous collaborator. Extremely generous, extremely considerate of the process, very understanding of time limits and deadlines.'

Detailed communication, careful listening and early planning are key, but an acute understanding of how the other person works and what makes him tick is a vital ingredient – and one that perhaps can't be taught. 'There are people in life that you just have an instant connection with, and that was the case when I met Kenneth Branagh,' the composer explains. 'We're both of Celtic background, we both share a very strong sense of humour, and I have discovered over the years that I really can read his mind and vice versa. You save an awful lot of time when you're ahead of someone's thoughts.'

In 1997, Patrick Doyle was diagnosed with leukaemia. He continued to compose throughout his treatment and made a full recovery. In 2007, his film scores were performed by the London Symphony Orchestra and Chorus at the Royal Albert Hall in a special 'Music for the Movies' concert held in aid of Leukaemia Research UK. Featuring appearances from British acting royalty, including Thompson, Dench and Jacobi, it was directed by Branagh, who was a leading force in staging the event. This may go some way towards explaining Doyle's comment: 'What I really appreciate about Ken is his constant loyalty and his friendship. We've been through a lot and for the record it's a highly unusual thing to have a director in this business who you've spent almost thirty years working with. I'm a very lucky man.'

 ## Collaboration History

*Henry V* (1989)

*Dead Again* (1991)

*Much Ado About Nothing* (1993)

*Mary Shelley's Frankenstein* (1994)

*Hamlet* (1996)

*Love's Labour's Lost* (2000)

*As You Like It* (2006)

*Sleuth* (2007)

*Thor* (2011)

*Jack Ryan: Shadow Recruit* (2014)

*Cinderella* (2015)

*Murder on the Orient Express* (2017)

 ## Suggested Playlist

*Henry V*, Opening Title

*Henry V*, Non Nobis, Domine

*Dead Again*, The Headlines

*Much Ado About Nothing*, Overture

*Much Ado About Nothing*, Sigh No More, Ladies

*Mary Shelley's Frankenstein*, The Escape

*Hamlet*, In Pace

*Hamlet*, Oh, What A Noble Mind

*Hamlet*, Sweets to the Sweet Farewell

*Love's Labour's Lost*, Victory

*As You Like It*, Under The Greenwood Tree

*As You Like It*, Violin Romance

*Sleuth*, The Visitor

*Sleuth*, Rat In A Trap

*Thor*, Thor Kills the Destroyer

*Thor*, Chasing the Storm

*Thor*, Can You See Jane?

*Jack Ryan: Shadow Recruit*, Ryan, Mr President

*Cinderella*, A Golden Childhood

*Cinderella*, Courage and Kindness

*Cinderella*, Who Is She?

*Murder on the Orient Express*, Justice

*Murder on the Orient Express*, Poirot

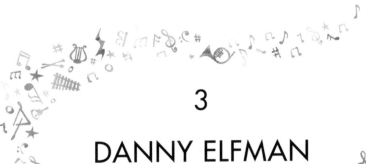

# 3

# DANNY ELFMAN
# AND TIM BURTON

*'Just two weird guys,*
*working on our own'*

*I*f you had to describe a Tim Burton film, words like 'eccentric', 'quirky', 'gothic' or 'weird' might spring to mind. *Edward*
*Scissorhands*, *Batman* and *Charlie and the Chocolate Factory*, for
example, all possess a distinctive glint in their eye, one that allows the
audience to revel in the macabre within a realm of playfulness. In a partnership spanning more than three decades, Danny Elfman has provided the
perfect musical complement to Burton's twisted tales and stylised visuals.
They have worked on seventeen films together, with Burton taking the role
of director for all but two of them, serving as producer for *The Nightmare*
*Before Christmas* and, more recently, *Alice Through the Looking Glass*. Their
next collaboration as director and composer is the live-action remake of
Disney's *Dumbo*, due for release in 2019. They are unique outsiders who
have been embraced by audiences and major film studios. Just as a Tim
Burton film often feels instantly recognisable, there is a definitive Elfman

sound, involving scampering percussion, a soaring chorus and a real sense of mischief. As the director long since acknowledged, Elfman's music plays a vital role in his movies: 'It is as important as some of the actors or anything, if not more important. Danny is an actor in the films.'

Burton and Elfman pursued their careers along slightly tangential paths, with the director starting out in animation and the composer in performance art and later as frontman of the new-wave band Oingo Boingo. Their respective backgrounds have proved highly influential as definers of their style and technique, and indicate a shared creative outlook: as Burton once said, 'It's trying to show that it's all just a process and that there are different ways to approach things. I think both you and I hate categorisation. People are always trying to stick you in a box and say, "Oh, he's in a rock band. Now he's a composer, but he only composes *this* kind of stuff."'

They are self-confessed fans of horror films from the 1950s, 1960s and 1970s and this common ground has added to their shared sensibilities, but while their partnership appears, from the outside looking in, to be a true meeting of minds, Elfman does not allow himself to get too comfortable: 'I'm surprised every time I get a call again to do another film. I don't ever expect to do his next film. He will call if he's ready to call.' To date, there are only three films directed by Tim Burton that haven't been scored by Danny Elfman: *Miss Peregrine's Home for Peculiar Children* (2016), apparently due to scheduling conflicts, *Sweeney Todd* (2007), because it used Stephen Sondheim's existing music, and *Ed Wood* (1994) – more on that later.

Elfman may be linked most often with Burton in the world of film scoring, but his most recognisable composition is undoubtedly the theme from hit television show *The Simpsons*. Of his four Academy Award nominations, only one is for a Tim Burton film – the somewhat underrated *Big Fish* – and the others make for a varied list: *Good Will Hunting*, *Men in Black* and *Milk*, demonstrating his music-making has far more breadth than a quirky paint-by-numbers model. Having collaborated with other respected directors like Gus Van Sant, Sam Raimi and David O. Russell, Elfman remains one of the hardest working and most open-minded composers around. In his view, 'Writing the score is the easy part. Getting into the director's head and understanding their psyche is what's hard. But that's what you need to do. You have to be half-composer, half-psychiatrist.'

⁓

Elfman's first film-scoring project for Burton was his first feature-length film, *Pee-wee's Big Adventure* (1985), about Pee-wee Herman's quest to retrieve his stolen bicycle. For those unfamiliar with Herman, he's a besuited man with a red bow tie and a childlike demeanour, portrayed by the comedian Paul Reubens. Pee-wee comes across as both endearing and strangely sinister, and the persona was so engrained in American popular culture that it was Pee-wee, not Paul, who received a star on the Hollywood Walk of Fame. His later fall from grace, when Reubens was arrested and charged with indecent exposure, was a remarkable, scandal-fuelled affair.

In the mid 1980s, Danny Elfman was the lead singer and songwriter in Oingo Boingo. The band, initially called The Mystic Knights of the Oingo Boingo, had been founded by Danny's brother Richard in the early 1970s, with leanings towards performance art, a world that Danny was well versed in, having worked in an avant-garde cabaret musical theatre group called Le Grand Magic Circus. He had never trained as a composer but had taught himself to transcribe and write music, and in 1980 Richard asked him to score a film he was directing, *The Forbidden*

*Zone*, based on the band's performances. That was Elfman's main experience of composing for the cinema before he met Tim Burton.

Burton had received early acclaim at the age of fourteen when he won first prize for his designs for an anti-litter campaign, resulting in his posters covering rubbish trucks in his district of Burbank, California. Disney Studios, which were down the road, sponsored him to attend the California Institute of the Arts, and one of his short films, *Stalk of the Celery Monster*, impressed Disney so much they offered him an animation apprenticeship. His first assignment, in 1981, was *The Fox and the Hound*, and his directorial debut was an animated short called *Vincent*, narrated by the horror-film actor Vincent Price, who would go on to play the inventor in *Edward Scissorhands*. Burton had written to his childhood hero with his idea for the short film and was overwhelmed at the response: '[Price] was so great and supportive, and even though it was a short film, he helped get it made. That was my first experience in this kind of world, and it was a really positive one. It stays with you forever.'

*Vincent* caught the attentions of Warner Bros., as did Burton's follow-up short at Disney, *Frankenweenie* – which would receive the feature-length treatment decades later – and the twenty-five-year-old animator landed himself the role of director for the new Pee-wee Herman movie after writer Stephen King, the master of horror, recommended *Frankenweenie* to a Warner Bros. executive, who showed it to Reubens. Not one to follow convention, Burton asked Elfman to score it. The composer recalled, 'I knew who Pee-wee was 'cos I'd seen Paul Reubens perform at The Groundlings and I thought he was great. I had no idea who Tim was, of course. Nobody did. When I met him, it was like, "Why me? Why would you want me to do a score? That's crazy." Tim was like, "I don't know. I've seen your band and I think you could do it." It was kind of that simple.' Burton explained his reasons to Elfman, admitting,

'I always thought you were very filmic in some way. I don't even know what that means! There was a strong narrative thrust to what you were doing. And it was theatrical. Also, because I hadn't made a feature-length film yet, I just responded to your work.'

With a first-time director and a self-taught composer, there was a lot of learning on the job, but despite the daunting challenge, their freshness offered up a blank canvas for creativity. Elfman cites Nino Rota and Bernard Herrmann as his two main influences on this score, specifically the Italian composer's films with Federico Fellini. The result sounds assured, in particular 'Breakfast Machine', which is full of now-trademark Elfman quirks, and is best experienced with the film to appreciate the sound effects that accompany Pee-wee's morning routine to the full. There is a circus feel to the music as the breakfast is prepared by bizarre inventions, creating a joyful atmosphere of chaos. Elfman recruited Oingo Boingo guitarist Steve Bartek to orchestrate his music – the two have gone on to work on over fifty scores together – and he credits the veteran composer Lennie Niehaus, a regular Clint Eastwood collaborator, who conducted this score, with steering him in the right direction.

Burton acknowledged Warner Bros. for surrounding him with an experienced crew while taking a chance on both him and Elfman. He can still recall his first impressions of Elfman's music for *Pee-wee's Big Adventure*: 'Hearing the music played by an orchestra was probably one of the most exciting experiences I've ever had. It was incredible and so funny to see Danny because he'd never done anything like that.'

~

*Pee-wee's Big Adventure* was a secure hit for the studio and despite appearing on some critics' 'worst films of the year' lists, it's become something of a cult favourite. Its financial success led to Warner Bros. hiring Burton to direct *Batman*, but the next Burton–Elfman collaboration was an episode of the revitalised television series *Alfred Hitchcock Presents*, called 'The Jar'. This allowed Burton to flex his horror and suspense muscles, and for Elfman to pay homage to his hero Herrmann. Their next film project together was **Beetlejuice** (1988), a deliciously madcap affair about a bio-exorcist ghost, played with gusto by Michael Keaton.

The score is a perfect fit, exuding cheekiness and menace with a melting pot of styles, including tango, waltz and calypso, that nestle well with the soundtrack songs by Harry Belafonte. The main titles don't start so much as they swerve around a corner towards you, pick you up and drag you along for the journey. The music feels free, even unhinged at times, and indicates how the director and composer worked at this period. Elfman recalled, 'The interesting thing about [the early films] for me was that there was no template to turn to, [Burton] didn't put a temp score in because they were really un-temp-able.' With the absence of musical steers or stabilisers, Elfman was able to take the cues in whichever direction he saw fit and then present his ideas to the director.

While *Beetlejuice* was Burton's second feature-length film, it was Elfman's fifth project: 'I had four films between Tim's early films, so *Pee-wee*, *Beetlejuice* and *Batman* was one, five and ten. Tim would say, "How are you doing all these films in between these movies?" and I'd go, "If I didn't, I couldn't do *our* movies, I have to learn." So that's how I learned. Every time I got in front of an orchestra, I was really hungry for it at that point and I wanted to try something new every time.' The likes of *Scrooged* and *Big Top Pee-wee* helped to get his name known, but *Beetlejuice* brought his style to the attention of mainstream audiences. Some of the more traditional critics were bemused by the energy and dynamism of Elfman's score, suspicious of his rock-band background, but many embraced him because his music mirrored the film so well.

Tim Burton and Danny Elfman while working on
*The Nightmare Before Christmas*, 1993.

This film provided a learning curve for the director too, demonstrating just how important it is to have music that fits – as well as reinforcing his already mixed feelings of working with major studios: 'There was a weird incident with *Beetlejuice*. We did some test screenings without the score, and the film got some really low marks. Then we showed it with the score and it got really high marks, and one of the things people liked from these test screenings was the score. But then somebody at the studio said that the score was "too dark", which was odd because these are the people who live and breathe by these audience research screenings and here they were contradicting the only positive thing from the screening.'

Cast your mind back to a time when superhero films weren't ten a penny at the box office. Before the Avengers assembled, before various Spiderman webs, and before the Dark Knight trilogy, there was Tim

Burton's *Batman* (1989), his first big-budget movie. 'A first for him, a first for me,' Elfman commented, before explaining that the director had had to fight the composer's corner for Elfman to score the film: 'Nobody wanted me on the film but Tim. It was the hardest and most difficult experience of my career.' Burton's unwavering support for the composer paid off, as did his refusal to back down over the casting for the lead role. The producers were wary of hiring Michael Keaton, an actor better known for comedies, but Tim stuck to his guns and the rest is history.

Despite the added pressure to perform, and the challenge of creating an 'action' score, the main theme is considered one of Elfman's best. Burton had asked for a dark, orchestral score, and this certainly fits the bill, starting eerily before gathering pace and power, with a robust performance by the orchestra as they hurtle towards the final cymbals. When compared to the typical crash-bang-wallops of many superhero scores, it is a classy affair, and rightly received a Grammy Award. *Batman* was a box-office hit, one of the first films to earn $100 million in its first ten days of release, and it changed the face of superhero movies with its blend of darkness and action. It was also one of the first films to offer two soundtracks, with music by either Elfman or Prince: Burton had originally asked Prince to write two songs for specific scenes, but the so-called 'Purple One' ended up writing more. On reflection, the director is not convinced: 'I don't think those songs work. It doesn't have anything to do with Prince's music; it has to do with their integration into the film.'

Elfman's music, however, fitted well, and the two returned for *Batman Returns* (1992), with the director agreeing to the role on the condition he would have more creative control. It was another financial success but received some criticism for veering further into darker and more violent realms. Burton enjoyed working with Elfman's themes for the characters, especially for Michelle Pfeiffer's transformation from Selina Kyle into Catwoman, and the composer has a soft spot for the music he wrote to accompany the Penguin's death, admitting it can bring him to tears despite the oddity of the scene, as Danny DeVito's character is lowered into the water by baby penguins. Yet while they are fond of particular cues with the benefit of hindsight, at the time it was a strained scoring process: they were working with a major studio and a larger budget, and the associated pressures that can come with both. The hits kept coming, but the cracks were starting to appear in their relationship.

⟿

In between *Batman* and *Batman Returns*, Burton and Elfman worked on **Edward Scissorhands** (1990), arguably their definitive collaboration, in which both director and composer are at the height of their powers.

Tim Burton has made no secret of his unhappy childhood and a feeling from an early age that he didn't belong. As a teenager, he had drawn a picture of a thin man with blades for fingers. Fast-forward a decade or so, and he developed a gothic fairy tale about this character with Caroline Thompson, then a young novelist, who would go on to work with Burton on *The Nightmare Before Christmas* and *Corpse Bride*. He has said this was a personal tale for him and while he was resolute about many aspects of the film – such as sticking with his first choice, Johnny Depp, to play the title role despite studio pressure to choose another actor – he gave Elfman space to create the score. His faith in the composer's instinctive ability removed the need for detailed directorial briefs and discussion: 'Danny and I don't even have to talk about it. We don't even have to intellectualise – which is good for both of us, we're both similar that way.' Some composers would struggle without specific steers or clarity from the director, but while leaving Elfman to get on with the job might feel like a risk on Burton's part, such a hands-off approach clearly works for these two.

Elfman has described the lack of a temp score as a good thing – leaving him free to jump into the composing process without pre-conceptions: 'I rarely end up writing anything I set out to write. *Edward Scissorhands* certainly was a case in that I didn't know where to begin, so I just started writing these melodies and I came up with these two themes and I sat down with Tim and I played them both and he says, "Oh, I like them both." We tried to talk about which one is Edward's theme and then we [each] said, "Both of them!" And I said, "Yeah, why not, there's no rules" – there's absolutely no rules – and so it's a weird score. No other characters have a theme. Edward has two! There's no rhyme or reason to it, it just felt right. Now later I can go, "Well, one ties in with the story and one ties in with the fairy tale and this character and that character", but there was no intention of this at the time. It just happened.'

He has described scoring *Edward Scissorhands* as 'a really cool process of being left alone with Tim. Nobody was watching over our shoulders, nobody even seemed concerned that we were even writing a score or working on the music. We were just two weird guys working on our own, under the radar and everything.' The resulting music feels magical but melancholic, creating an otherworldliness from the opening 'Introduction' to the much admired and imitated 'The Grand Finale', which twinkles like a mournful 'Somewhere Over the Rainbow'. Elfman's trademark mischief is toned down to make way for the awestruck wonder of the chorus, and it makes for a beautiful stand-alone listening experience.

It's not surprising that this is one of the composer's favourite scores, but he wasn't wholly convinced at the time: 'When I wrote that score, my first feeling about it was that I'd done a terrible job. It didn't feel like a real score, and I thought I was going to get killed for that one. And that's why it's more amazing that it became one of my most well-known scores, but I really had no confidence whatsoever that I'd done a good job on it till years later, starting to hear other renditions of it and then I thought maybe it was OK because it seems like I'm hearing all kinds of variations on it. But I didn't feel that as I was writing it, and I don't actually think I ever do, so I'll settle for: "It came out interesting."

'By the way, that's the highest compliment I've ever heard Tim say about one of his own works: "I think this one came out pretty interesting."'

As with *Edward Scissorhands*, Tim Burton came up with the concept for *The Nightmare Before Christmas* (1993) when he was younger. In this case it was a poem, written when he was working at the Disney animation department. He considered making the tale of Jack Skellington, a resident of 'Halloween Town' who finds himself in 'Christmas Town', into a children's book and showed his storyboarded ideas to animator Henry Selick. However, Burton then left the studio and plans were halted, but he returned to the idea later on, and produced the stop-motion animation film with Selick in the director's chair due to Burton's commitments on *Batman Returns*.

*The Nightmare Before Christmas* feels very much a part of the Tim Burton world in its aesthetic and tone despite not being directed by him. That the film is a dark delight and remains a seasonal favourite in many households is due in no small part to Elfman's catchy tunes that toy with musical expectations of what sounds 'scary' and 'Christmassy', often playing the two off against each other. The 'Overture' starts with festive brass and bells before taking us somewhere altogether more eerie, and the driving pulse of 'Christmas Eve Montage' is reminiscent of his *Beetlejuice* score with its runaway pace, but the songs, featuring lyrics and rhymes by Burton, offer the stand-out moments. Elfman provided the vocals for Jack, capturing his confusion at stumbling into Christmas in 'What's This?', and the hummable motif of this cue is woven throughout the score. Another highlight is 'Town Meeting Song', when Jack describes the festive celebrations he's seen, and this features the composer's favourite lyric by Burton: when the townspeople wonder what might be wrapped up in a present box, one speculates 'perhaps it's the head that I found in the lake'.

The process of bringing the film to life is significant in demonstrating Elfman's contribution to Burton's projects; this is definitely not a case of tacking the music on at the end. Burton had originally asked *Beetlejuice* writer Michael McDowell to expand his three-page poem into a feature-length script, and when he wasn't happy with the results, he decided to approach the story from a musical angle, and brought Elfman on board.

'We'd worked together so much that it didn't matter that we didn't know what we were doing; at least we knew each other,' states Burton, recalling, 'I would go over to his house and we would just treat it like an operetta . . . where the songs are more ingrained in the story. I would begin to tell him the story and he'd write a song; he wrote them pretty quickly, actually, at least the initial pass on them.' The two fleshed out a storyline, the composer started to write the songs, and then Selick and the animators began to create the visuals – all before Caroline Thompson was involved in writing the screenplay.

During this process, Elfman drew parallels between his continued role as frontman of Oingo Boingo and the character of Jack Skellington:

'I was the singer and the songwriter, so, in a way, I was the king of my own little kingdom. But I desperately wanted out. I wanted something else. So as I was creating songs for Jack and writing those parts, I was also kind of writing from my own heart and where I felt at that time . . . I wrote most of everything in about thirty days with Tim, but when I recorded the demos with him, I finally said, "Tim, I almost couldn't bear it if someone else was singing these songs." And he said, "No, don't worry. They're your songs."'

~

The scoring process for *The Nightmare Before Christmas* sounds creatively fulfilling but the jumbled chronology of storywriting, composing, scriptwriting and production strained Burton and Elfman's partnership further. A break may have been on the cards, given the build-up of creative pressures both were under. As Burton later reflected, 'I think he was mad at me from *Nightmare*. *Nightmare* was hard because between Danny, Henry and Caroline, we were like a bunch of kids, fighting.' When Burton started planning his next project, the biopic of real-life director Ed Wood, who was considered by some as 'the worst director of all time', he didn't ask Elfman to come along for the ride, but invited Howard Shore instead. In an interview during the post-production of *Ed Wood*, Burton said, 'We're taking a little vacation from each other.'

As the composer put it two decades later, 'We had a two-year falling-out which I think was inevitable with our personalities.' Audiences can be grateful that it turned out to be a short-term separation. Looking back, it might have been a necessary hiatus: 'We lucked out because we talked early on. We used to joke we'd end up like Bernard Herrmann and Alfred Hitchcock and they had a famous falling-out which they never patched up. And then that happened with Tim and me. But I had a very volatile temper and Tim is particularly strange and it was a fantastic lesson for me, because I think it had to happen somewhere, and it happened there. It was at the end of *The Nightmare Before Christmas*. I'd worked two years on it, and was then finishing *Batman Returns* in the middle of that, and it was really an intensive time.'

When they reconciled a few years later, Burton was similarly realistic about the split: 'I think it was just one of those times when, like in any relationship, we just needed a break, and it was probably good for all of us. Danny works with many different people, so I think every now and then it's worth trying something new, and I enjoyed working with Howard.'

For Elfman it taught him an important lesson about the collaborative process and how personality and ego can interfere, and about his own methods of dealing with creative conflict and pressure: 'When I feel these feelings coming up, I try to imagine I'm looking at myself through a telescope. I back it up, back it up again, back it up a third time, and look again at what's happening. Nine out of ten times I'll go, "Oh, you know what, from back here it looks like a serious thing for a minute. It doesn't look like it's worth all that, is it?" And you go, "No, it's not." That lesson has helped me many times. I think it's part of the process of a volatile personality learning to adjust to reality.'

While they share similar outlooks and sensibilities, this partnership may differ from the others in this book because Elfman is a performer first and a film composer second. Would many lead singer-songwriters be willing to take direction or constructive criticism without putting up a bit of resistance? Other composers here have acknowledged their position within the film-making process and deferred to the vision of the director, but the Burton–Elfman partnership appears to be on more of an equal footing – and, for that very reason, one with more potential to become fractious.

Elfman, however, is not alone in offering this significant analogy for their relationship: 'It's like being in a marriage. Lots of little things can happen and we had many little things in those years and then something is the straw that breaks the camel's back and it's usually not that big of a thing. Someone says something the wrong way and suddenly there's just a huge fight. And the thing with Tim and I was very much like family; I've had huge fights with my brother but he's my brother, and when the chips are down, that's who I turn to. And losing Tim for that period of time, I'd actually felt like I lost a brother, a sibling, and it felt when we came back together like, "Oh, patched things up in the family, it's as it should be."'

❧

Based on the trading card series of the same name, *Mars Attacks!* (1996) was a homage to sci-fi B-movies like *It Came from Outer Space* and Ed Wood's *Plan 9 from Outer Space*. Another composer had already been hired but, according to Elfman, Burton had a change of heart: 'The story I got from the producer was they were sitting in a hotel together and *Batman Returns* came on. They both watched it and at the end Tim said, "Danny should be doing this film, shouldn't he?" And the producer called my agent, my agent called me and said, "Would you ever speak with Tim again?" Probably the next day I was on a plane for Kansas, and we met in a coffee shop and just said, "We won't speak of this." There was no talking it out, Tim's not that way, he's just like, "Let's never speak of this again, let's just start from scratch." And we did.'

Cue sighs of relief all round for fans of the Burton–Elfman alchemy, although, admittedly, *Mars Attacks!* is unlikely to be considered the zenith of their collaboration history. Receiving a mixed reception from critics despite a starry cast, it has retained some cult appeal, and it allowed the composer to experiment with music to match the B-movie setting, incorporating the theremin and wearing its Herrmann influences, most notably *The Day the Earth Stood Still*, with pride.

Over the next two decades, the pair honed their skills and styles, creating gothic, supernatural and fantasy worlds of varying dramatic proportions with the likes of *Sleepy Hollow* (1999), *Big Fish* (2003), *Corpse Bride* (2005), *Dark Shadows* (2012) and *Frankenweenie* (2012). Burton has spoken of their ability to communicate through visuals rather than words, in that he shows Elfman footage which describes the emotions he wants the score to convey, but it shouldn't be assumed that the partnership has evolved into a near telepathic state. Speaking to the *Guardian* in 2013, Elfman said, 'People expect us to have some invisible shorthand but it never gets any easier. Tim is just as complex now, maybe more so. Every time I play music for him I'm as nervous as I was that first occasion. Countless times, I've played something and watched him just put his head in his hands and start pulling at his hair. With Tim, I've never been unhappy with where we've ended up, but most of the time we've had to spiral around quite a bit to get there.'

Nearly a decade after the success of *Batman* and *Batman Returns*, Tim Burton tried his hand at contributing to another existing franchise, this time **Planet of the Apes** (2001). The reboot performed well at the box office but received criticism for its lighter tone in comparison with the 1968 film and suffered from production issues and last-minute script rewrites. The film was still being completed while Elfman was working on the score, so he was faced with the task of composing without seeing the final footage. He avoided the pressure of comparison with the original score by choosing *not* to nod to Jerry Goldsmith's music, but instead continued with his tried-and-tested method of scoring a handful of key scenes in the film, testing those cues, and then filling in the gaps in chronological order.

The end result doesn't feel like a typical Elfman score, with its militaristic and efficiently layered sounds. He admits he still enjoys pushing himself and seeing where his music-making will take him: 'I'm fuelled by the chance to do something I haven't done before. Not every film can, not every score can, but I try, and every now and then I succeed . . . So I just wait for those moments where I could do something and it's like, "Oh, that felt different." I never know if it's good, but it's different.'

⋙

Expectations were especially high for Burton's version of Roald Dahl's much-loved **Charlie and the Chocolate Factory** (2005) because comparisons would inevitably be made with the popular 1971 film version, *Willy Wonka & the Chocolate Factory*, but Elfman appears to have thrived on the pressure because his songs and score are bold, joyful and not a little bit bonkers. Burton, Elfman and Depp were also working on the stop-motion animation *Corpse Bride* at the same time, and the composer may have found it rejuvenating to juggle the two projects, especially as this was the first time since *The Nightmare Before Christmas* that he was contributing songs and his vocals to a Tim Burton film. He experimented with different styles for the songs about each of the children taking part in Wonka's factory tour, as they are serenaded away following their demises. Layering his voice to portray all of the Oompa Loompas, he serves up a hyperactive Bollywood pastiche in 'Augustus Gloop' and the woozy pop number 'Veruca Salt', and he veers towards the unhinged with rock guitar and harmonies *à la* Queen in 'Mike Teavee'.

Other highlights from a soundtrack that fizzes with flavour include 'Wonka's Welcome Song', a guaranteed earworm featuring high-pitched voices and a fairground organ that welcomes the guests to the factory. On its own, it's a cracking singalong tune, but it's worth experiencing with the film to witness puppets bursting into flames and a suitably macabre denouement, and it earned Elfman and screenwriter John August a Grammy nomination.

Elfman's and Burton's next project together was based on another popular children's book, this time *Alice in Wonderland* (2010) by Lewis Carroll. The visual nature of the story and the surreal characters within it must have been catnip to Burton, and his take on the beloved tale picked up the Academy Awards for Best Art Direction and Best Costume Design. Boasting a starry cast including Anne Hathaway and Burton regulars Johnny Depp and Helena Bonham Carter, this is the director's highest-grossing film to date, and was one of the biggest box-office successes of 2010. Elfman delivered a strong score, with 'Alice's Theme' as a particular highlight, but the composing process was a tricky one, because again he had to score scenes that were not yet finished, so that Burton could fit them into last-minute edits. You wouldn't know that from the finished product, however, because Elfman is more than adept at conjuring a score to accompany a journey of peril and wonder into the unknown.

Burton and Elfman stepped into the unknown, with regard to their partnership, with the small-scale biographical drama *Big Eyes* (2014). Elfman is accustomed to scoring lower-budget films – for every *Fifty Shades of Grey* and *The Girl on the Train* he'll compose *The End of the Tour* and *Promised Land* – but nearly three decades into his collaboration with Burton this was quite a change of pace. A refreshing one, according to him: '*Big Eyes* is like nothing I've done with [Burton] in the sense that the scale was so small, the budget was so limited. I mean, of course, the budget wasn't big on *Pee-wee's Big Adventure*, but it's been a while since I've had a really tight low budget with Tim and it was fun!'

*Big Eyes* is the most recent of Tim Burton's directorial projects to receive the Danny Elfman scoring treatment. Fans of their partnership had been concerned at the news that Elfman was not scoring *Miss Peregrine's Home for Peculiar Children* (2016), a job that went to Mike Higham and Matthew Margeson, but that was due to scheduling and availability as opposed to an *Ed Wood*-style separation. At the time of writing they are working on Disney's live-action remake of *Dumbo*, which has the potential to be in the same league as their finest collaborations.

While they have had clashes, there is a bond between them that has allowed the relationship to flourish over three decades. Burton clearly acknowledges how Elfman's scores capture and embody the emotions of his films, and recognises that 'The music is the guide post, it's the tone and the context.' He trusts the composer to create a complementary sound world to his vision, while Elfman attributes their successful alchemy to a shared outlook: 'I think it's a skewed sensibility about life in general. We grew up on many of the same influences. We're both horror, fantasy kids growing up in Los Angeles, raised on movies. When I met Tim, one of my great film idols was the actor Peter Lorre and his was Vincent Price, and I realised later that that would actually define much of our relationship: Vincent Price was usually the master and the torturer, and Peter Lorre was always the tortured soul! But that says a lot about us: the same cheesy wonderful Roger Corman horror films that starred these two actors were among our favourites growing up.

'But why it clicked? There's no real answer to that.' And that may be exactly how they want to keep it.

## *Collaboration History*

*Pee-wee's Big Adventure* (1985)

*Beetlejuice* (1988)

*Batman* (1989)

*Edward Scissorhands* (1990)

*Batman Returns* (1992)

*The Nightmare Before Christmas* (1993), produced by Tim Burton

*Mars Attacks!* (1996)

*Sleepy Hollow* (1999)

*Planet of the Apes* (2001)

*Big Fish* (2003)

*Charlie and the Chocolate Factory* (2005)

*Corpse Bride* (2005), co-directed by Mike Johnson

*Alice in Wonderland* (2010)

*Dark Shadows* (2012)

*Frankenweenie* (2012)

*Big Eyes* (2014)

*Alice Through the Looking Glass* (2016), produced by Tim Burton

 ## *Suggested Playlist*

*Pee-wee's Big Adventure*, Overture (The Big Race)

*Pee-wee's Big Adventure*, Breakfast Machine

*Beetlejuice*, Main Titles (Beetlejuice)

*Beetlejuice*, The Aftermath

*Batman*, The Batman Theme

*Batman*, Love Theme

*Edward Scissorhands*, The Grand Finale

*Edward Scissorhands*, Ice Dance

*Batman Returns*, Birth of a Penguin Parts 1 and 2

*Batman Returns*, Selina Transforms Parts 1 and 2

*The Nightmare Before Christmas*, What's This?

*Mars Attacks!*, Introduction and Main Titles

*Sleepy Hollow*, Main Titles

*Planet of the Apes*, Main Titles

*Planet of the Apes*, Ape Suite #2

*Big Fish*, Sandra's Theme

*Charlie and the Chocolate Factory*, Wonka's Welcome Song

*Charlie and the Chocolate Factory*, Augustus Gloop

*Charlie and the Chocolate Factory*, Veruca Salt

*Corpse Bride*, The Piano Duet

*Corpse Bride*, Tears to Shed

*Alice in Wonderland*, Alice's Theme

*Dark Shadows*, We Will End You!

*Frankenweenie*, Mad Monster Party

*Frankenweenie*, Happy Ending

*Big Eyes*, Who's the Artist?

*Big Eyes*, Margaret

*Alice Through the Looking Glass*, Looking Glass

# 4

# MICHAEL GIACCHINO
# AND J.J. ABRAMS

*'It's a weird thing to meet someone
and feel so immediately in sync.'*

Of the five films J.J. Abrams has directed, four of them – *Mission: Impossible III*, *Star Trek*, *Super 8* and *Star Trek: Into Darkness* – have been scored by Michael Giacchino. There is a valid reason why Giacchino didn't work on the fifth: that was *Star Wars: The Force Awakens* and the unbreakable laws of the cinematic universe dictate that composing duties for the galaxy far, far away belong to John Williams and to John Williams alone. That is, unless we're in the galaxy for a stand-alone spin-off film, in which case someone else can use the musical force. Step forward Giacchino with *Rogue One: A Star Wars Story*, directed by Gareth Edwards.

Four out of five is a pretty good innings, yet the Abrams–Giacchino partnership extends further than Abrams' feature-length directorial projects. The two have collaborated on television dramas *Alias*, *Lost* and *Fringe* and Giacchino has scored films co-produced by Abrams such as *Mission: Impossible – Ghost Protocol* and *Star Trek Beyond*.

Regular collaboration is vital to their individual and collective successes, Giacchino has explained: 'I work with the same guys over and over again. Rarely do I step outside of the circle of directors who I love dearly, because I know that they're always going to challenge me, they're always going to ask something different and allow me to do something different.' (Giacchino has a characteristically engaging manner; he almost pinches himself with glee when talking about his work.)

Giacchino has achieved the rare feat of avoiding being typecast as a composer, due partly to the variety of the projects he's worked on with Abrams, but also thanks to his long-term relationship with Disney Pixar. His first feature-length score for them was *The Incredibles* in 2004, the first of his five collaborations to date with director Brad Bird, and he's also notched up various projects with directors Matt Reeves, Colin Trevorrow, Pete Docter and the Wachowksis.

Abrams' regular collaborators include Bryan Burk, the co-founder of his production company Bad Robot, writers Alex Kurtzman and Roberto Orci, *Lost* co-creator Damon Lindelof, actors Greg Grunberg and Simon Pegg, and editors Maryann Brandon and Mary Jo Markey, but he has not forged a long-term working partnership with any other composer. Unlike most directors, Abrams also composes music for the screen and has created or contributed to themes for television shows including *Alias*, *Lost* and *Person of Interest*. In fact, his first film job, aged sixteen, was as composer and special-effects contributor on a sci-fi horror called *Nightbeast* (1982). As a result he perhaps has a greater appreciation than most of the power of music on screen, describing a score as 'a window into the scope, the scale, and the soul of the piece'.

Abrams and Giacchino were born just over a year apart, in June 1966 and October 1967 respectively. The young Jeffrey Jacob Abrams, as the son of a television producer and executive producer, had the more natural entry to the world of film-making, but he has described a tour of Universal Studios with his grandfather as the moment when he caught the movie bug. He was eight years old, and from then on he started to experiment with his parents' camera. Film music was also a source of fascination for him, and he described on the eve of the release of *Star Wars: The Force Awakens* how, as a young boy, 'I would lie on the floor of my room with headphones on, listening to scores of films, often films I hadn't seen, and very often scores that John Williams had written. And those were full stories; I would close my eyes and I would see the whole story. I'd look and see what the cue was called, and put together what was happening. I got it right sometimes and not quite right other times, but the music told the story.'

Giacchino was also in thrall to Williams' work from an early age, and credits his parents for allowing him to follow his passions: 'They said . . . "You want to make movies? Here's my movie camera, I have no idea how to tell you what to do with it, but let's try and figure it out."' In his delightful acceptance speech at the Academy Awards in 2010 when he won the Best Original Score Oscar for the Disney Pixar hit *Up*, Michael said, 'I know there are kids out there that don't have that support system, so if you're out there and if you're listening . . . if you want to be creative, get out there and do it, it's not a waste of time. Do it!'

Giacchino studied film production at the School of Visual Arts in New York before focusing on music at the prestigious Juilliard School, and his early training may be an indicator as to why he and Abrams are such a successful collaborative unit: just as Abrams' first-hand experience as a composer informs his response to scores, Giacchino's background of making home movies followed by studying the craft of film-making allows him to fully appreciate the roles of a producer and director.

The result is a true meeting of minds, with each acknowledging the skills that the other brings to the project.

Abrams was in college when he wrote and sold his first screenplay – the 1990 comedy *Taking Care of Business*, released in the UK under the somewhat outdated title of *Filofax*. Before the dawn of the new millennium, he had co-written the weepy Bruce Willis sci-fi hit *Armageddon* and successfully pitched the first of his television hits, the college drama *Felicity*. Co-created by Abrams and Matt Reeves, it ran for four seasons and Abrams was an executive producer, writer of seventeen episodes, director of two, as well as the theme music co-composer. It's safe to assume he doesn't do things half-heartedly.

Giacchino took a slightly less conventional route, earning his stripes in the world of video games. He built a strong reputation within this increasingly competitive market, and soon he was working on high-profile projects such as DreamWorks Interactive's *The Lost World: Jurassic Park* PlayStation game (one of the first console titles to be recorded with an original live orchestral score, an experience that must have been invaluable when he signed up to score *Jurassic World* years later) and the *Medal of Honour* series, created by Steven Spielberg.

However, Giacchino had immersed himself so well in the world of video games that he was at risk of being pigeonholed: 'No one would hire me in TV because they thought I was a video-game guy, and it took somebody like J.J., who listened to the music that I did for the games, to say, "Oh, we should work with him."' Abrams had been developing a new show, *Alias*, with college friend Jesse Alexander, a huge video-games fan who recommended Giacchino. After their first meeting, Abrams knew he didn't need to contact any other composer: 'It's a weird thing to meet someone and feel so immediately in sync. Our life experiences were very different on one hand, but on the other hand we both loved movies in exactly the same way, so we hit the ground running.'

Abrams was quick to recognise Giacchino's ability, cementing their initial connection: 'It got to a place incredibly early on during *Alias* when I realised that I didn't have to spot music at all with him. Michael just knows where music should and shouldn't be.' The acclaimed show about a double agent ran for five seasons, but the duo had to wait a few more years for their breakthrough.

～

*Lost* (2004–10) is consistently considered to be one of the greatest television dramas of the 2000s. Years later, Giacchino still sounded slightly incredulous at the impact of the story about a group of survivors from a plane crash on a mysterious tropical island: '*Lost* went to this place that I never expected. People all over the world know and love the show. I had never experienced that with something that I had worked on before, and it was really eye-opening.'

Spanning six seasons, *Lost* attracted 16 million viewers an episode at its peak and was garlanded with critical praise and industry recognition. The pilot alone won four Emmy Awards, including Outstanding Directing for a Drama Series, for Abrams, and Outstanding Music Composition for a Series (Dramatic Underscore) for Giacchino. The composer shared his first impressions: 'I remember thinking, "Wow, what am I possibly going to do with this?" but I always have that experience. I think I don't know what I'm going to do, but then when I watch it, I feel something and then I know what to do. It takes watching it and feeling something. The worst situation you can get yourself into is when you watch something and feel nothing. Those are the films you have to stay away from, because then it's very difficult for me to write anything in that situation.'

Giacchino was given creative freedom and enjoyed constructing what would become a definitive sound world, complete with unsettling sliding trombones and the use of plane fuselage within the percussion: 'I could do whatever I wanted, and I felt that it was important to do something that didn't sound like it was just another jungle score: "They're in a jungle, so it's got to sound like a jungle, and we're gonna have shakuhachi flutes." I didn't want to do any of that nonsense. I wanted to come up with some strange ensemble that felt odd, that I could do weird things with. We had strings, trombones, harp, piano, percussion – and the percussion was very strange! – and that was it. We used that same ensemble for the entire run of the show. I remember someone at the studio said, "Shouldn't we have flutes?" and I said, "No, if you do that, you're going to make people comfortable, and this is a show about making people uncomfortable."'

This sparse ensemble created by Giacchino provided original music to respond to the twists, turns, plot developments and introductions – or demises – of the vast cast of characters. He estimates that he composed around 52 hours of music, because he scored a new episode every week, choosing not to 'library' the show (use pre-existing recordings) unlike many other television dramas: 'It was important, I felt, that this should have an original score on every episode because the stories were so complicated and you never knew when a new character was going to come up ... It was a sort of psychotic opera that was being created and everyone needed to have those themes. It was a way of helping the audience track everything – and helping me track everything!'

Another bold decision by Giacchino was to score the music on a scene-by-scene basis, responding to the drama as it unfurled directly in front of him, without any spoilers or tip-offs from the writers and producers: 'I refused to read any scripts, I didn't watch any early cuts. I

J.J. Abrams and Michael Giacchino during a scoring
session for *Star Trek: Into Darkness*, 2013.

would get the show, and I would start with scene one and go in order . . .
I had three days to do it, generally: you write and orchestrate it in three
days, and on the fourth day you're recording it, and on the fifth day
maybe you get a day off, and then the next week you're doing it all over
again. It's a hectic schedule but it was important for me to be reactive
with the music because I felt like it's a show that the audience is reacting
to constantly, something that is being thrown at them, and I wanted the
music to reflect that anxiety or that sadness or whatever it called for.'

Giacchino clearly relishes opportunities for spontaneity, finding in it
both the chance to be creative and to have fun, and his unconventional
approach paid off with *Lost*: choosing to remain in the dark about such
a twist-filled storyline, in which most things the viewer is led to believe
later turn out to be untrue, resulted in far greater musical impact, with
the score reflecting the audience's reaction as the story unfolded.

For their first film collaboration, Abrams and Giacchino were entrusted with a franchise that was already known and loved by millions – themselves included. ***Mission: Impossible III*** (2006) was the first of a series of reboots that the two would work on together, based on original stories and characters that were already dear to them. Giacchino commented, 'It is very strange to be in a place where the people who grew up loving those shows that other people made are now in charge of remaking them for a whole new audience', but Abrams felt his television work on *Alias* and *Lost* had prepared him to inherit the action spy franchise, and he described the former as being little sister to *Mission: Impossible III*'s big brother. The composer was faced with the challenge of working with one of film's most instantly recognisable pieces of music, Lalo Schifrin's original theme.

He decided to bite the bullet and give Schifrin a call: 'He was a fan of *The Incredibles*, so he was very sweet and offered to meet me for lunch. So we met and I was talking with him and he says to me, "I really love *The Incredibles*", and I was like, "Yes, but I want to talk about *Mission: Impossible*. I'm really worried about doing this movie, and I just want to talk to you about what should I do and what shouldn't I do." And he looked at me like I was crazy! From my point of view, it was like asking someone if I could marry their daughter, and it was a very nerve-racking thing for me, but he was the sweetest person and just said, "Go have fun with it!" and I did.'

The earlier *Mission: Impossible* films had been scored by Danny Elfman and Hans Zimmer, adding yet more pressure for Giacchino, but with Schifrin's blessing he had the confidence to approach the existing theme on equal terms, a skill that would serve him well in future reboots, although he describes his work in a typically modest fashion:

'I wanted his music to live amongst my music, and not just feel like we were slugging it in whenever we needed to have something punchy happen. I wanted – and I don't think I succeeded – but I wanted to write music that lived up to what he did, and could live alongside it, which was a daunting task.' The resulting score runs the gamut of emotions, from the plaintive piano and romantic strings in 'Reparations' to the ballsy action of 'Helluvacopter Chase', and it's evident how much fun he had with the existing music in cues such as 'See You in the Sewer' and 'Schifrin and Variations'.

When the film was released, Abrams explained why Giacchino was his only choice of composer for his leap from television to cinema: 'For some reason Michael and I see things very similarly. Whether it's his commenting on a cut or a story point or a scene, or my commenting on a theme, we always push each other.' Their discussions about the score would often involve a keyboard – played by the director: 'I start to play around with things. Music is so important to me and I'm incapable of doing the kind of magic Michael does, but I definitely like to express it, try to get it out so I can find things.' Abrams would communicate his ideas in this manner, with words and music, then Giacchino would record versions of temp tracks and deliver them for use during the edit, so the score 'was informing the cut of the film as much as the other way around'.

Since *Mission: Impossible III*, Giacchino has earned a reputation as a worthy inheritor of iconic film scores. Jerry Goldsmith's music for *Planet of the Apes* was bequeathed to him for the reboots *Dawn of the Planet of the Apes* (2014) and *War for the Planet of the Apes* (2017) – and, incidentally, Abrams has described the original *Planet of the Apes* as the film that changed his life. Giacchino has also been given the keys to two of John Williams' musical kingdoms: *Jurassic Park*, for films *Jurassic*

*World* (2015) and *Jurassic World: Fallen Kingdom* (2018), and, perhaps even more daunting, *Star Wars* for *Rogue One: A Star Wars Story*. Big shoes to fill is an understatement, but Giacchino has gained recognition from fans and critics for balancing creativity with a genuine respect for the original material. The same can also be said of Abrams, as both men have approached the challenge of remaking, or rebooting, film franchises with a strong appreciation of the original.

❧

One franchise in particular stands out due to its long-standing success in both television and film, and its revered musical legacy by great composers including Jerry Goldsmith and James Horner, not to mention the impeccable TV theme by Alexander Courage: *Star Trek*.

As his work on *Mission: Impossible III* was coming to an end and he heard whispers about **Star Trek** (2009), Giacchino found it hard to believe he might actually be involved in a reboot of this cherished series, in what would be the eleventh film in the franchise. *Star Trek* is nothing short of a cult phenomenon – after all, few popular shows can boast their own constructed language – and for over more than half a century, Trekkies have been treated to a variety of television series, spin-offs and films about the USS *Enterprise*.

A fan from childhood, the composer tried to keep a clear head during initial discussions: 'As with anything, until it happens, I try not to get too excited about it, because anything goes south in this town very quickly ... but I have to say, J.J. has great instincts and a great track record ... It's no wonder they went to somebody like him to take it, respect it, but also do something different with it.'

Abrams' aim was to bring the story back to the basic elements that had made the show popular in the first place and, along with writers

Roberto Orci and Alex Kurtzman, he created an origin story for James T. Kirk and Spock, albeit one with an alternate timeline. Fittingly, Abrams showed early footage of his first *Star Trek* in the same screening room in Paramount Studios where, as a thirteen-year-old, he had watched *Star Trek: The Motion Picture* along with his television producer father when it was unveiled to a select audience by director Robert Wise.

Giacchino initially struggled under self-imposed pressure, aware that he was inheriting the *Star Trek* baton from a range of composers who had each contributed an individual vision to the franchise. He felt the need to honour their work in his music: 'When I first started working on *Star Trek*, it was the hardest thing I had ever done because there were all these expectations, many of them fabricated in my own head . . . I wrote about twenty themes . . . and each and every one of them may have been nice musically, but just never felt like our *Star Trek*.' He would play his work to the director, who shared his concerns: 'J.J. kept saying, "I like it but it doesn't feel like *our Star Trek*", and we were all struggling to figure out what was "our" *Star Trek*. We didn't know because we were so hung up on everything that came before that was *Star Trek*.'

With both director and composer at a rare creative impasse, it took another regular collaborator, co-producer Damon Lindelof, to offer a new perspective: 'He said, "Think about this as a story between two people who meet, become the best of friends and then are going to spend the rest of their life together on these incredible adventures. They're going to get to know each other and they're going to not be able to live without each other by the end of it." . . . And at that point I just let go of everything that was *Star Trek*.' The resulting score was hailed by Abrams, and Giacchino recalls feeling that the whole experience was a 'huge lesson for me'.

Listening to the music now, there's no hint of the internal battle the composer went through. Two highlights – 'Enterprising Young

Men' and 'That New Car Smell' – are so self-assured, with their brass fanfares and triumphant resolutions, it's hard to believe he felt any pressure at all. Another piece, 'Labor of Love', is the heart-breaking musical accompaniment to a scene when the USS Kelvin is being attacked. First officer George Kirk sacrifices himself to ensure his wife and child survive and Giacchino chose to focus on the personal sadness rather than pen a typical 'action' cue.

However, there remained the matter of the original television theme. Should Giacchino incorporate the famous tune within the score, as he had been able to do with Schifrin's work in *Mission: Impossible III*? He discussed it at length with Abrams: both wanted to include it somehow, but felt that it didn't fit into the actual film that they were making. As Giacchino puts it, 'It's a very particular type of theme and it needs a certain sort of scene to work and we just didn't have that.' Their solution was to use it for the end credits, which gave them the freedom to 'do it as big as we've ever heard it and make it a celebration of what *Star Trek* is and where it came from . . . There's a hint of the opening tunes in one cue, but it's just a hint – and then at the end you get this huge version of that Alexander Courage theme which I love so much, and it was fun to mash that up with my theme as well. It was just our way of saying thank you to those guys who did that show.'

One aspect of Giacchino's approach wasn't wholly appreciated by the fans, however: 'If you know anything about my soundtrack CDs, they all have these crazy titles that my music editors and I come up with. We do insane, funny titles that are puns, and I remember after the *Star Trek* album was released, on some of the message boards there were some arguments about whether or not I should have done that on *Star Trek*. People were saying, "Does he not take this seriously? This is *Star Trek*!"'

Each to their own. For many, the wordplay within Giacchino's scores is a delight. Playful, goofy, sometimes smart and mostly ridiculous – think 'Nero Sighted' from *Star Trek*, 'Brigadoom' from *Star Trek: Into Darkness* and 'A Swarm Reception' from *Star Trek Beyond*, and that's just the tip of the pun iceberg. Perhaps part of his strength is that he doesn't take his job too seriously, or rather he knows to remind himself to keep enjoying it. He may however have learned a lesson from the Trekkies when he named the music for *Rogue One: A Star Wars Story* because the official titles are comparatively conventional, although he couldn't resist creating an alternative track listing, including 'Takes One to Rogue One' and 'Live and Let Jedi'.

It may be tempting to dismiss Abrams' and Giacchino's film collaborations as a series of reboots or inventive contributions to blockbuster franchises rather than anything more ambitious, but one original project suggests otherwise. *Super 8* (2011) is a stand-alone, coming-of-age film that pays homage to the sci-fi films of their childhood, most notably the works of Steven Spielberg such as *E.T.* and *Close Encounters of the Third Kind*. How perfect, then, for their inspiration to get on board and co-produce it. Looking back, it might seem as though that was all part of their plan, but Giacchino is keen to point out that that's far from the truth. When Spielberg attended the recording sessions, 'J.J. and I would look at each other and go, "Can you believe this? This is crazy that we're sitting here and Steven's right over there. He's standing right there!"'

The story of teenagers who are filming a homemade movie when a mysterious presence enters their town, *Super 8* is a nostalgic sci-fi thriller, made with love. Abrams showed Giacchino the script early on and they discussed the music, scene by scene, before shooting had even begun.

Just as the film pays tribute to Spielberg, the score is clearly imbued with respect for John Williams' 1980s works, and with its sense of childlike wonder and nostalgia, it feels instantly recognisable. Of all his film scores for Abrams, this is perhaps the most satisfying as a stand-alone listen, combining sweeping, cinematic orchestral cues with an openly referential nod to Williams, and it feels like a heartfelt thank you to both the director and composer. As Giacchino said of Spielberg, 'We all have people that as a kid we looked up to and loved, and never did I think I would be lucky enough to actually be there working with him.' When he conducted a performance of one of the score's stand-out tracks, 'Letting Go', at his own fiftieth-birthday concert at the Royal Albert Hall in October 2017, the footage of his early films accompanied the music, and watching a young Giacchino and friends re-enacting scenes from *E.T.* and *Raiders of the Lost Ark*, it was clear how personal a project this film had been.

The composer had a cameo role in *Super 8* as Deputy Crawford, and another on-screen part in Abrams' later film, *Star Wars: The Force Awakens*. Some believed the director cast the composer as First Order Stormtrooper FN-3181, seen briefly during the opening sequence of the film, as an apology for not hiring him to score the movie, but this would not have been necessary. Giacchino explained in 2015, before the release of the film: 'As a fan of the series, I want to go into the theatre and hear *Star Wars* music, which means John Williams needs to write it.' Abrams will be back behind the camera for Episode IX, due for release in December 2019, and there must be a likelihood of Giacchino being involved in some capacity, either on or off the screen.

❧

Williams' and Spielberg's long-standing collaboration has thrived despite – or perhaps because of – the composer's great achievements with other directors, most notably with George Lucas on *Star Wars*. In the same vein, Giacchino's extensive extra-curricular work, particularly on Disney Pixar films, has arguably injected freshness into his partnership with Abrams. Both director and composer are talented storytellers, adept at developing existing franchises as well as creating original works, and more unusually they both have experience in film-making and film scoring so each has a proper understanding of the different skills required. Abrams has described his composing work as a 'hobby' in comparison to Giacchino's, yet his respect for movie music is central to their collaboration because he fully appreciates the significant role it plays: 'If you remove the music the film doesn't exist the way it does normally, but if you remove the film you can still feel the story.'

Perhaps most crucially, Abrams and Giacchino treat their audiences with respect, which is particularly vital in the world of remakes and reboots as they are inheriting stories and characters that are already beloved. They are self-confessed movie nerds who can relate to passionate fans because they belong in that world too, and they are mindful of not abusing their position of power by adding to the canon of, say, *Star Trek*, with a story that doesn't meet expectations. As the composer notes, 'We still have this very boyish quality about what we do', and the combination of this with their impressive work ethic and limitless creativity is extraordinarily powerful.

On stage for Giacchino's fiftieth-birthday concert, Abrams described the composer's scores as a 'litmus test' for him as a director: if the music doesn't fit a scene, he knows the scene is at fault and needs more work, not the other way around. Giacchino attributes their harmonious and successful partnership to an honesty pact they made, which allows them to raise and address concerns: 'When you stop listening to other people, when you think that, no, your idea is the only good idea, that's when you find yourself in trouble because that is a terrible place to be. J.J. and I have talked about this many times over the years and … we will always be honest with each other, no matter what it is, because it's not personal … Sometimes it will change, sometimes it doesn't, but it's being able to have that open dialogue that is so important.' Abrams praises the ease of their working relationship: 'There is an absolute fluidity, there's an effortlessness to it.' Giacchino pinpoints the end result: 'True collaboration is what makes things better.'

 ## *Collaboration History*

*Alias* (2001–6), created by Abrams

*Lost* (2004–10), co-created by Abrams

*Mission: Impossible III* (2006), directed and co-written by Abrams

*Fringe* (2008), co-created by Abrams

*Cloverfield* (2008), co-produced by Abrams

*Star Trek* (2009), directed and co-produced by Abrams

*Super 8* (2011), directed, written and co-produced by Abrams

*Mission: Impossible – Ghost Protocol* (2011), co-produced by Abrams

*Star Trek: Into Darkness* (2013), directed and co-produced by Abrams

*Star Trek Beyond* (2016), co-produced by Abrams

 ## *Suggested Playlist*

*Alias* (season 2), Inferno

*Lost* (season 4), There's No Place Like Home

*Lost* (final season), Moving On

*Mission: Impossible III*, Reparations

*Mission: Impossible III*, See You in the Sewer

*Cloverfield*, Roar! (Cloverfield Overture)

*Star Trek*, Labor of Love

*Star Trek*, That New Car Smell

*Star Trek*, Enterprising Young Men

*Super 8*, Letting Go

*Super 8*, Mom's Necklace

*Mission: Impossible – Ghost Protocol*, Kremlin with Anticipation

*Star Trek: Into Darkness*, Kirk Enterprises

*Star Trek: Into Darkness*, The Kronos Wartet

*Star Trek Beyond*, Thank Your Lucky Star Date

*Star Trek Beyond*, Night on the Yorktown

# 5

# BERNARD HERRMANN
# AND
# ALFRED HITCHCOCK

*The Masters of Suspense*

'Iconic' is a word that's used far too frequently in the world of cinema but when it comes to Alfred Hitchcock and Bernard Herrmann's working partnership, nothing else does it justice. Theirs is the benchmark for every creative collaboration between director and composer, and perhaps its dramatic and abrupt ending serves to add to its status within movie-making history.

From *The Trouble with Harry* (1955) to *Marnie* (1964), Hitchcock and Herrmann, more often known as Hitch and Benny, worked on eight films together. Compared with some of the other collaborations in this book that may seem like a small number, but their impact and influence is vast. At the centre of their partnership is the unmatched sequential triumvirate of *Vertigo* (1958), *North by Northwest* (1959) and *Psycho* (1960), each considered to be among the finest films ever made. The score for one of their films, *The Birds* (1963), was far from typical, so the composer was credited as sound consultant, and what would have been their ninth project, *Torn Curtain* (1966), turned out to be their last when Hitchcock famously turned up at the recording sessions, argued with Herrmann and dismissed the orchestra.

The names of few directors and composers have become adjectives, but even if you've never seen a Hitchcock film, you'll know about the shower scene in *Psycho* and *those* jabbing strings. You would have some idea about what a 'Hitchcockian' movie would entail: a suspense, a thriller, a story in which the audience should expect the unexpected. Plot twists, distractions, an ordinary character placed in an extraordinary situation, often involving mistaken identity – these are some of the Hitchcockian tropes that film scholars and movie fans alike have discussed over the decades, and continue to do so. In the same way, a 'Herrmannesque' score conjures intrigue and melodrama, foreboding and dread, and is able to evoke romance laced with disquiet. Many composers owe Herrmann a debt; nobody could do 'unsettling' quite like him.

Hitchcock and Herrmann had very different personalities, and neither was famed for being the easiest to work with. The director has been described as an urbane East Londoner with an unflappable disposition and a meticulous approach to film-making. He was very much the boss of his films and had a reputation for testing his actors, likening them to 'cattle' in a series of interviews with the director François Truffaut, as well as being particularly controlling of his leading ladies. Herrmann was considered to be difficult, even cantankerous, and he tended to be in conflict with various studios, directors and other composers throughout his career. However, he was fiercely loyal to his friends, and those who knew him well viewed him as a real softie.

Despite their contrasting personalities, the two shared a similar sense of humour and an appreciation for the macabre. As their bond became closer, Hitchcock would invite Herrmann to see early rushes of his films, something he had never done before with composers. Instead of writing out detailed notes and musical directions, he would trust Herrmann to write something that would not just fit the scene, but elevate it.

This is the key to their success: they both understood the importance of music to a film and recognised that it could be used to express what is not overtly shown or spoken. With that, they redefined cinema.

Putting Herrmann's collaboration with Hitchcock to one side, the composer would still have an enviable scoring CV, considering it's bookended by two masterpieces: *Citizen Kane* (1941) and *Taxi Driver* (1976).

We have Orson Welles to thank for Herrmann's movie music. The composer started out scoring radio plays for Welles, and after seven years of radio conducting, he moved to Hollywood at the request of the director. The studio behind *Citizen Kane* was keen to get the thirty-year-old newcomer on the cheap, but Welles insisted he received the same fee as one of the most sought-after composers of the time, Max Steiner, and straight off the bat with his debut film score, Herrmann received an Oscar nomination for Best Dramatic Score. Yet his music for *Citizen Kane* wasn't victorious that year, beaten by another of his nominated scores, *The Devil and Daniel Webster* (also known as *All That Money Can Buy*).

Herrmann worked again with Welles on *Jane Eyre* (1943), and during the 1940s the composer divided his time between work for the concert hall and the cinema. His great passion was conducting and he preferred to call himself a 'composer who worked in film' rather than a 'film composer'. This was less to do with snobbery than his firm belief that music is music, whatever medium it's written for. He would do his own orchestrations for film scores and was known for being very exacting with his musicians, often pushing them to their limits. The results, such as *The Ghost and Mrs Muir* (1947), *The Day the Earth Stood Still* (1951) and *The Snows of Kilimanjaro* (1952), speak for themselves – and didn't he know it. According to Herrmann in an interview with Royal S. Brown, the director 'only finishes a picture 60 per cent. I have to finish it for him.'

Hitchcock had been keen to work with Herrmann about a decade earlier but conflicts with schedules or studios prevented it. He wanted the composer to score *Spellbound* in 1945 but that role went to another legend of Hollywood's golden era, Miklós Rózsa, earning him the first of his three Best Original Score Oscars. However, Hitchcock had not been a fan of what he thought was intrusive music, despite the praised and much imitated use of the theremin as a byword for suspense, and Rózsa did not work for him again. Hitchcock had no qualms about cutting people, cast or crew, out of his projects.

Herrmann was also unable to work on *To Catch a Thief* in 1955, so Lyn Murray took on scoring duties, and when Murray couldn't do the following film, he put Herrmann forward. The rest is history.

⁓

Hitchcock understood his audience. He placed them at the centre of each film, and chose to control or manipulate them, ensuring that they never got too comfortable. Ultimately, though, he knew his role was to entertain. One of the few directors to successfully combine mainstream and orthodox film-making with visionary and experimental methods, he was skilled at adapting to, and at times leading, cultural trends and the adoption of new technologies.

In his fifty years as a film director, from 1926 to 1976, Hitchcock navigated his way through a fascinating period in cinema history, over-coming two seismic shifts in the industry: first the transition from silent films to 'talkies', and later the arrival of television sets in family homes. With the advent of the gogglebox weakening the big film studios' grip on entertainment and popular culture, Hitchcock cannily became a television personality of sorts, hosting the series *Alfred Hitchcock Presents* (later *The Alfred Hitchcock Hour*) for which Herrmann would score seventeen episodes. Hitchcock literally put himself into his work. With his film cameos and television introductions, his face became well known. People would go and see 'an Alfred Hitchcock film' solely because his name was attached to it.

On leaving school, Hitchcock became a draughtsman in an engineering firm and studied art at the University of London. His first work in film was as a title designer, before he moved into directing. He carried the aesthetics of silent cinema into the new sound films, telling Truffaut that he viewed silent films as the 'purest form of cinema', a belief that would inform the use – or absence – of music in his later work. In fact, John Williams, who scored Hitchcock's final film, *Family Plot* (1976), maintained in 2012 that one of the main things he had learned from the great director was knowing when to stop the music and let the silence in.

Hitchcock had made over twenty films in Britain before he was invited to Hollywood by producer David O. Selznick, and his first American movie, *Rebecca* (1940), was a success, receiving eleven Academy Award nominations and winning two, for Best Picture and Best Cinematography. It was the first of five Best Director nominations for Hitch, although curiously, considering his lasting appeal, he was never to win.

The director worked with some of the greatest film composers, and collaborated on four projects each with Franz Waxman, including one of his finest, *Rear Window* (1954), and with Dimitri Tiomkin: *Shadow of A Doubt* (1943), *Strangers on a Train* (1951), *I Confess* (1953) and *Dial M for Murder* (1954). These working partnerships should be viewed as successes by the very fact the composers were asked back on several occasions, but the chemistry that Hitchcock would find only with Herrmann was lacking.

━━◈━━

When Hitchcock and Herrmann finally got to team up their individual careers were already at a high, and together they would climb even higher. The composer liked the idea of scoring a black comedy, and **The Trouble with Harry**, a macabre tale about a corpse that won't stay buried, appealed to him.

Perhaps underrated in comparison with their later collaborations, this is a very British film within an American aesthetic. Herrmann provided a light score, suggesting a disturbing humour within the rural Americana of the setting. He repurposed existing music from CBS radio series *Crime Classics* and incorporated his own original cues, artfully playing with western musical tropes by shifting them ever so slightly, leading the audience down a seemingly familiar path before arriving somewhere unsettling. The Prelude toys with musical expectations before throwing the audience off-kilter, hinting at the half-diminished seventh chord that would become the celebrated trademark for *Vertigo* and *Psycho*.*

The dark humour of the film was far more appreciated by audiences in England and France than in the United States, and it was the only one of Hitchcock's Paramount films not to make a domestic profit on initial release. However, audiences were much more receptive to it when

---

* Herrmann's favoured half-diminished seventh is a minor seventh chord, with the fifth flattened, e.g. C – E flat – G flat – B flat. Tension and dynamism is driven by the embedded tritone (C – G flat), while consonance and stability is provided by the minor third (C – E flat) and the perfect fifth (E flat – B flat).

Alfred Hitchcock and Bernard Herrmann while working
on *The Man Who Knew Too Much*, 1956.

it was re-released in 1963 in a double-bill with *The Man Who Knew Too Much*. Tonally, it was a strong influence for the *Alfred Hitchcock Presents* television series, for which the director asked that his introductions and conclusions were written in the style of this film.

Viewed alongside their later projects, *The Trouble with Harry* might not be a 'typical' Hitchcock film or Herrmann score but it provides hints about how the two gelled. The director classed it as one of his favourite scores and, in 1968, after the two had gone their separate ways, Herrmann wrote the short suite *Portrait of a Hitch*, incorporating sequences from the score, and dedicated it to the director.

Their second collaboration was a remake of Hitchcock's 1934 film ***The Man Who Knew Too Much*** (1956), which had at the time relaunched his career as a skilled thriller director, but which he felt was 'the work of a talented amateur'. With bigger budgets and decades more experience in his favour, Hitchcock set out to retell the tale of kidnappers, a mysterious murder, an assassination attempt and a holidaying couple caught up in it all.

This is one of his most musical films in the sense that music has more of an overt presence: Doris Day's on-screen rendition of 'Que Sera, Sera' won the Best Original Song Oscar and reached number two in the Billboard charts, and the film's memorable climax takes place at a concert at the Royal Albert Hall in London, where a shooting has been planned to accompany the crash of a cymbal.

Some critics view this as a masterclass in the dramatic use of music, and there are hints of their core collaborative 'sound' taking shape, such as rising and falling arpeggios in key scenes. However, due to the presence of other music and the decision to keep Arthur Benjamin's 'Storm Cloud Cantata' from the original film in the concert scene, this was not Herrmann's greatest chance to shine. The composer orchestrated and expanded the piece, and while he didn't make his mark over the whole score as he would for later Hitchcock projects, he appears in the film as the conductor of the London Symphony Orchestra at the concert. He reportedly won over the orchestra with his musical knowledge and tales of Hollywood. After shooting the film, the musicians presented him with a volume about the orchestra's history, with the inscription 'To Bernard Herrmann, the Man Who Knows So Much'.

*The Wrong Man* (1956) quickly followed, based on the true story of Christopher Emmanuel Balestrero, who was framed for crimes he didn't commit – a definitive Hitchcock trope. Henry Fonda plays the lead role of Manny, a bass player at New York's Stork Club, and elements of the score reflect the character's jazz background. The film opens in the club with a terrifically – and misleadingly – jaunty prelude, the sort of music you'd want to greet you as you open your front door in the morning, at the start of what will turn out to be a fantastically successful day. Not quite so for the rest of the film. It is a sombre tale, at times unrelenting and frustrating, and the score reflects this.

❧

By the time Hitchcock and Herrmann worked on what would be considered one of their masterpieces, they had developed a mutual respect and understanding. A story of obsession and control, *Vertigo* received mixed reviews on release and wasn't a huge commercial success, but it is now widely viewed as the finest and most revered Hitchcock film. In 2012, it topped a critics' poll of the greatest films of all time, published in *Sight and Sound* – the official British Film Institute magazine. This honour had previously been held by *Citizen Kane* every decade since 1962. Director Martin Scorsese considers *Vertigo* to be one of his favourite films and its impact is far-reaching, including technical styles such as the famous use of the 'dolly zoom', which created the impression of vertigo for the viewer.

James Stewart's detective, John 'Scottie' Ferguson, develops a fear of heights and is forced to retire when a colleague falls to his death. He is then hired by an old friend to watch his wife, Madeleine, who has reportedly become possessed by the spirit of her ancestor, Carlotta Valdes. Then it appears that Madeleine has died, and Scottie is tormented by her death. Months later he sees a woman with a resemblance to her, and he tries to recreate the dead woman through her.

Hitchcock had wanted Herrmann to listen to Norman O'Neill's score for J. M. Barrie's 1920 play *Mary Rose* as part of his preparation, and apparently the studio went to great lengths to track down the only remaining vinyl recording in England for him, but a more prominent musical influence on the final score is the 'Liebestod' from Wagner's opera *Tristan und Isolde*, especially in the famous 'Scène d'amour', a piece full of anguish, where love and obsession collide. Despite the title, it feels unsentimental, more a reflection of Scottie's state of mind as he confesses his love for the woman known as Madeleine, continually building up to dangerous heights.

Herrmann's score for *Vertigo* is the longest for any Hitchcock film. He was in a position of freedom compared to composers who had worked for Hitchcock before: when the director submitted his usual detailed notes to the sound department, he kept some of the scenes vague, adding that the sound requirements would depend on what music had been written. For someone so methodical, this indicates the faith he placed in Herrmann.

As with the following two films, Saul Bass designed the iconic opening titles, and Herrmann wrote the music to fit the visuals. Bass, himself an innovator who had previously worked with other great directors such as Otto Preminger, referred to Hitchcock as a 'master', and the titles prepare the audience well for the film, with disconcerting swirls and close-ups of an eye. The music matches perfectly, with foreboding arpeggios, and the spiralling music brings about its own sense of vertigo.

However, Herrmann knows when to scale back the anguish, and there is real economy in the music in another famous scene when Scottie follows Madeleine around the streets of San Francisco. Incidentally, Herrmann didn't think this was the best setting, and wrote the score with the heat of New Orleans in mind. It is a long scene with no dialogue, highlighting Hitchcock's skills in silent films, and when Scottie is watching Madeleine in the graveyard, the music, colours and editing form a perfect bond. It really is a masterclass in film-making.

~

From the dizzy heights of infatuation to a fast-paced thrill ride. Screenwriter Ernest Lehman set out to write the 'Hitchcock picture to end all Hitchcock pictures' and the tale of Cary Grant's advertising executive Roger O. Thornhill who is mistaken by a gang of spies for a US government agent, George Kaplan, is energetic, stylish and fun. More of an instant hit in the cinemas than *Vertigo*, **North by Northwest** was a strong influence on the James Bond series, and apparently Ian Fleming asked Hitchcock to direct the first film about 007. Imagine what might have been.

The opening sequence starts as a green image before Saul Bass introduces grids of thin lines, fading to the New York traffic reflected in a building and later to the busy streets, and Herrmann's 'Overture' brings it alive. Described by the composer as a 'kaleidoscopic orchestral fandango', it is repeated in various cues throughout the film, such as 'The Wild Ride', when Roger is driving to escape the clutches of James Mason's Vandamm and also 'On the Rocks', the famous showdown at the top of Mount Rushmore. MGM Studios had asked for a score in the style of George Gershwin, but Herrmann characteristically ignored the request, preferring South American rhythms to express the cat-and-mouse dance that takes place throughout the film. Yet it's not all frenetic, and the 'Conversation Piece' that features when Roger meets the beautiful Eve on a train to Chicago is dreamy and languid.

The music was composed and orchestrated in fifty-one days. As was Herrmann's style, he worked his way through the score from the beginning to the end of the film, sketching it out before writing a neat orchestral score in ink. It is a lean score, with only fifty-three minutes of music in a film lasting two hours, but it packs a punch. You'd be forgiven for thinking there is music during the famous crop-dusting scene, when Roger is pursued by a plane with nowhere to hide and take shelter, but there is none – another fine example of restraint on behalf of the composer and director.

<hr>

The famous story behind the shower scene in *Psycho* and the accompanying strings is that Hitchcock had asked for no score, but Herrmann wrote one anyway. The director had wanted to use just the sound of running water, and this would have been effective enough considering the shocking events unfolding on-screen, but the composer was convinced he could take it one step further. Storyboarded by Saul Bass and shot from a range of angles, this remains a truly disturbing scene, yet the addition of the controlled and inventive strings, played with such attack, heightens the dramatic impact: the high strings are prominent when the murder is taking place and the low strings take over after the killer has left. Hitchcock recognised how powerful the combination of visuals and music was and allowed himself to be proved wrong – on this occasion.

The director was mindful that the shower scene, one of the twists in the film, would be crucial to the film's success. The marketing campaign told audience members they had to arrive for the start of the film and this paid off because people would queue around the block to get a ticket. Equalled only by John Williams' *Jaws* theme as musical short-hand that everybody understands, those strings embody fear in film, and Hitchcock acknowledged Herrmann's contribution by placing the composer's name at the end of the opening credits, just before his own.

Another exercise in restraint, *Psycho* does not actually show much on-screen violence but allows viewers to piece the horror together themselves, 'designed to terrorise an audience, but only in their mind', as Hitchcock explained in an interview for television programme *Speculation* in 1969. The film was made on a low budget, in black and white, and Herrmann said he wanted to create a 'black and white' score to match, hence the sole use of strings. During the production, Hitchcock began to feel so despondent about the film that he considered splitting it in two and broadcasting it on his television show but Herrmann saw its potential and persuaded him not to, so we have him to thank for more than simply the music.

The Prelude invites the audience in with its beguiling speed and an intriguingly dreamy motif over the frenetic strings. Robert Ziegler, who has conducted live performances of the score to accompany film screenings, admitted at a Hitchcock study day at London's Southbank Centre in 2017 that when it comes to this particular piece, his direction to the orchestra is always to 'play faster'. The theme is repeated as Janet Leigh's character Marion Crane drives away with the stolen money, adding urgency to an otherwise static close-up of a woman at the wheel, and during the rainstorm that leads to her fatal decision to pull into Bates Motel.

Although the shower scene is cemented within our collective cultural compass, it is not the only example of complete synergy between visuals and score. Hitchcock was said to have described the editing process of private investigator Arbogast's death scene in terms of music. The sudden strings that accompany a shot from above, showing the killer rushing out of the bedroom, can still make audiences jump out of their seats. Yet again, *Psycho* shows the strength in silence: in a key scene directly after Marion's murder, there is no music or dialogue, and it makes for a compelling contrast to the strings and screams echoing in the audience's ears.

Despite the instantly recognisable parts of the score, Bernard Herrmann described another melody as the 'real *Psycho* theme': a simple three-note sequence in 'The Madhouse', when Marion Crane suggests to Norman Bates that his mother should be put into a home. The composer used it again in his final film score, during the end credits of *Taxi Driver*, because he viewed Robert de Niro's character, Travis Bickle, as another 'psycho' who would attack again.

*Psycho* did not receive unanimous critical praise on release but the public loved it and it was a box-office hit. Hitchcock commented in interviews that Herrmann's music was a large part of the film's success but some film critics believe that the cracks in their collaboration had already started to form by this point, because the composer had contradicted the director's initial instructions about the shower scene. The two were close enough for Herrmann to be able to convince the director to listen to his work and consider it for inclusion in the first place, but for Hitchcock, who was known to hold a grudge, it might have been a struggle to share the limelight.

At one point during the making of *Psycho*, Hitchcock apparently toyed with the idea of not using any music at all but incorporating solely sound effects, an experiment he tried with his next film, **The Birds**, considered by many to be his last great masterpiece. Herrmann was involved as a sound consultant and the avant-garde electronic sounds were created by Remi Gassmann and Oskar Sala on a device called a trautonium. The sounds are atmospheric and desolate, offering no explanation as to why the birds attack Bodega Bay, if anything creating more uncertainty.

A year later, the two worked together on **Marnie**, which would be their final completed collaboration. Described on the posters as a 'suspenseful sex mystery', the psychodrama starred Sean Connery and the current 'Hitchcock blonde', Tippi Hedren, as the eponymous heroine, a thief who trades on her looks to win the trust of employers, then robs them and changes her identity. The production was troubled for both director and composer, as Herrmann was separating from his second wife and Hitchcock's behaviour towards the lead actress was becoming too controlling. *Marnie* is not considered to be their finest film and it had a lukewarm reception on release, yet the music is well worth exploring for its confident, and at times complex, cues.

Herrmann recruited a much smaller ensemble than for *Vertigo*, a score that *Marnie*'s is often compared to, perhaps owing to their roles of conveying anxiety and inner turmoil. He paired the wind players and had four horns, harp and strings – the exact instrumentation of *The Trouble with Harry*, forming an unwitting symmetry to his work with Hitchcock. He composed themes that would serve to intensify or mirror the visual motifs on the screen, such as the colour red. Instead of creating leitmotifs to represent the characters, his themes portrayed emotions such as desire or jealousy. The 'Trauma' theme features in flashbacks to explain Marnie's mental state, used effectively in 'Red Flowers', when she sees a bouquet of red gladioli, and it is repeated to differing degrees of intensity throughout the film. The director provided one musical steer in the script, for the first horse-riding scene. Riding is Marnie's passion and Hitchcock wanted a crescendo of the main theme to show the 'real Marnie' – one that is passionate and warm, unlike her usual persona. It is reported that he wanted the music to 'surpass the quality of the *Spellbound* theme', referring to his earlier film, also about psychoanalysis. The Prelude starts in a tormented frame of mind before becoming more typically romantic, and there appears to be a struggle between anxiety and calm during the short cue, which ends with a return to the torment.

The film studio had asked for a hit tune to go with the score, as was the fashion at the time, because it was a useful way of marketing and bringing in extra publicity and revenue, but this was not Herrmann's style. When Hitchcock raised the matter, the composer was surprised and frustrated that the director was so willing to comply with the studio's demands. He managed to convince him otherwise, but *Marnie*'s poor box-office returns not only intensified the pressure on Hitchcock to deliver a hit, but may have added to a growing resentment towards Herrmann.

≈

There are various stories about the showdown between the director and composer but here's what we know: for Hitchcock's next film, the Cold War thriller **Torn Curtain**, he needed a box-office success. He succumbed to studio pressure to cast big stars Paul Newman and Julie Andrews, and yet again there was the demand for a hit song in the score, following in the successful footsteps of 'Lara's Theme' by Maurice Jarre for *Doctor Zhivago* (1965).

The times they were a-changing, and by the mid 1960s there were shifting expectations from both studios and audiences about what a film score should sound like. Pop sensibilities were filtering into traditional, sweeping scores and Herrmann's music for *Marnie* had not helped to draw in the crowds. Hitchcock wrote to him about his new project and, displaying an acute awareness about the new industry demands with regard to film scores, stated the need for 'a beat and a rhythm'. He asked the composer to be open to these new musical styles, with an ominous 'If you cannot do this then I am the loser.' Despite this seemingly clear message, there was evidently a lack of understanding between the two, which can't have been helped by the fact they were communicating via telegrams or intermediaries.

Hitchcock asked for a beat theme; Herrmann stuck to orchestral. To make matters worse, the director stipulated – again – that he did not want any music for the murder scene. What did the composer do? He attempted to repeat the tactic that had been so successful in *Psycho* and wrote a cue for the killing of the security officer Gromek. Whether Herrmann went against instructions owing to impudence, ego or sheer creative will, we'll never know, but for Hitchcock, this was the last straw.

On that fateful recording session in March 1966, Hitchcock arrived – there is some debate as to whether he was invited or expected – and, unsurprisingly given his request for a more stripped-back score, he did not react well to seeing a full fifty-seven-player ensemble. An argument broke out between Hitchcock and Herrmann in front of the orchestra, who had earlier burst into spontaneous applause after recording the film's title music, a show of support that, considering what happened next, must have been some solace to the composer. The director berated him, telling him it wasn't the sort of score he'd asked for, and cancelled the recording session. Herrmann wanted Hitchcock to listen to what they had already recorded, but he refused, making the unheard-of decision to shut down the sessions halfway through: the musicians would need to be paid anyway, so logic would dictate they might as well record the rest. Herrmann, with his characteristic temper and damaged pride after this public dressing-down, did not give up without a fight. The confrontation continued over the phone, sealing the end of the collaboration.

Hitchcock then hired Surrey-born composer John Addison, who had scored *Lucky Jim*, *A Taste of Honey* and *Tom Jones*, to take over scoring duties, and the new *Torn Curtain* main theme does indeed sound younger, with hints of John Barry, but the film was neither a critical nor commercial success, and the music could not have rescued it. You can now watch the film with either Herrmann's or Addison's scores and compare the two, which is well worth doing if you ever need reminding how music can influence your perception and enjoyment of a film. Herrmann's prelude is a solidly rousing affair, immediately pulling the audience in with its pace and intrigue – no wonder the orchestra applauded at the recording sessions – and for a cue that was specified *not* to be composed, 'The Killing' was certainly written with some gusto.

Some stories claim that Hitchcock and Herrmann never spoke again, but Norma Herrmann, the composer's third wife, recalls meeting the director in Universal Studios in the late 1960s or early 1970s and that her husband gave Hitchcock a copy of his opera of *Wuthering Heights*. That sounds like an attempt at a truce, but apparently Herrmann admitted to his wife that he had been pleased by the scaled-back appearance of the director's offices, as that indicated his reduced status at the studios, and the composer was said to be delighted whenever a later film of Hitchcock's was a flop. In a telling tale about their personalities, when Hitchcock was giving a talk at the University of Southern California and was asked whether he would work with Herrmann again, he said, 'Yes, if he'll do as he's told.'

After a galling dry period when the studios rejected him in favour of 'running with the kids', as in the younger composers with their hit songs and beat scores, Bernard Herrmann would find further success. In 1976, rising star director Brian De Palma wanted to make a Hitchcockian film, *Obsession*, and who better to score it than Herrmann? Soon, the young directors were chasing the creator of scores that had influenced their formative film-going experiences. Martin Scorsese hired Herrmann for *Taxi Driver*, he was in talks with Steven Spielberg shortly before he died – and he delighted in turning down the studios when they called him up to ask him back, telling them he had 'decided to run with the kids'.

The kids continue to show their admiration for Herrmann. Danny Elfman is a self-proclaimed fan – he's referred to the composer as 'my god' and he scored *Hitchcock* (2012), the biopic about the making of *Psycho*, while Quentin Tarantino used the ominous whistle from *Twisted Nerve* (1968) in *Kill Bill* (2003). Elmer Bernstein, a friend of Herrmann's, used some of the rejected *Torn Curtain* score in Martin Scorsese's remake of *Cape Fear* (1991), along with some of his music for the original 1962 film. Somewhat controversially, the 'Scene d'Amour' from *Vertigo* was used at length in the multi-Oscar-winning silent film *The Artist* (2011), so Herrmann continues to find new audiences and is still widely considered a master of film scoring.

Hitchcock meanwhile remains the master of suspense and all self-respecting directors owe him a debt. He released three films after the split with Herrmann – *Topaz* (1969), *Frenzy* (1972) and *Family Plot* (1976). He worked with Maurice Jarre on *Topaz*, to middling results, and dismissed Henry Mancini's score for *Frenzy*, replacing the composer with Ron Goodwin. None of the final three would match his earlier successes.

～

Clashing egos, miscommunication, buckling under studio pressures or simply a case of all good things coming to an end? Whatever ultimately led to their separation, at the height of their powers Hitchcock and Herrmann created some of the most influential and revered critical, commercial and artistic successes. Neither could recreate the magic with anyone else, yet both were too stubborn to make amends.

The key to their collective alchemy, spanning just over a decade together, was their awareness of the power of music to bind the audience to the film. It was said they could read each other's minds to achieve the required results that would test the viewers by enhancing the emotional depth of a scene and adding elements of tension and unease. Together, they shifted the audience's perceptions about what music should, and could, add to a film.

In these aspects, they were ahead of their time, and Herrmann may have been even more pioneering in his attempt to assert himself on an equal footing with Hitchcock in an era when the director's word was law. This book shines a spotlight on so many contemporary collaborations in which the director and composer welcome an honest, two-way dialogue, but that relationship was rare in Hitchcock's and Herrmann's day. The composer made real headway because he was so confident of his talents and of what his music could bring to a film that he didn't accept every direction he was given. This is evident in game-changing successes such as *Psycho*, but ultimately led to the breakdown of a remarkable creative partnership.

##  *Collaboration History*

*The Trouble With Harry* (1955)
*The Man Who Knew Too Much* (1956)
*The Wrong Man* (1956)
*Vertigo* (1958)
*North by Northwest* (1959)
*Psycho* (1960)
*The Birds* (1963), with Herrmann credited as Sound Consultant

*Marnie* (1964)
*Torn Curtain* (1966), rejected score

 ## Suggested Playlist

*The Trouble With Harry*, Overture
*The Trouble With Harry*, A Portrait of Hitch
*The Trouble With Harry*, Autumn Afternoon
*The Man Who Knew Too Much*, Concert Overture
*The Wrong Man*, Prelude
*The Wrong Man*, Sanitarium
*Vertigo*, Prelude
*Vertigo*, Rooftop
*Vertigo*, Scène d'amour
*Vertigo*, The Nightmare
*North by Northwest*, Overture
*North by Northwest*, The Wild Ride
*North by Northwest*, Conversation Piece
*Psycho*, Prelude
*Psycho*, The City
*Psycho*, Temptation
*Psycho*, The Murder
*Marnie*, Prelude
*Marnie*, Marnie
*Marnie*, The Storm
*Marnie*, The Hunt
*Torn Curtain* (rejected score), Prelude
*Torn Curtain* (rejected score), Valse Lente
*Torn Curtain* (rejected score), The Killing

# 6

# JAMES HORNER AND JAMES CAMERON

*'It's like having a tango partner –*
*you've got to have absolute trust.'*

irector James Cameron and composer James Horner collaborated on just three films, but their partnership made a seismic
impact on the world of film-making, breaking box-office records
and redefining expectations of film scoring. They worked together on a
film a decade and each has had considerable influence: *Aliens* (1986) is
consistently ranked as one of the finest sequels ever made, while *Titanic*
(1997) boasts the best-selling primarily orchestral soundtrack of all time
and held the record as the highest-grossing film of all time – that is,
until the release of their final project, *Avatar* (2009). This was the first
movie to earn more than $2 billion worldwide, a feat later achieved by
its predecessor following its re-release in 2012 to mark the centenary of
the sinking of the RMS *Titanic*.

The staggering successes of this assorted triptych is the reason why
this chapter focuses on Horner's partnership with Cameron, despite the

composer's vast back catalogue – over a hundred film scores – including regular collaborations with other directors, such as Mel Gibson and Ron Howard. There will be a brief detour to assess Horner's seven film scores for Howard, in order to explore further his approach to film scoring, but if you're looking for a collaboration in which both individuals push themselves to their respective limits, that story belongs to Jim and James.

Sadly, following Horner's death at the age of sixty-one, their association as director and composer will only ever comprise *Aliens*, *Titanic* and *Avatar*. Horner's S-312 turboprop aircraft crashed into the Los Padres National Forest in California on 22 June 2015. An avid pilot, he was the sole person on board. His death was ruled an accident.

He had been due to start work scoring the *Avatar* sequels later in the year. Looking back at his illustrious career composing for the cinema, it began and ended with Cameron.

✌

Born just over a year apart, director and composer both earned their cinematic stripes with the independent film-maker Roger Corman – 'the Pope of Pop Cinema'. Corman's B-movies and horror films, made on tight time frames and low budgets, have acquired a cult appeal, and the people who worked their way through the ranks of Corman's studios have left an indelible mark on film history: he nurtured directors Francis Ford Coppola and Martin Scorsese and gave career breaks to aspiring actors such as Jack Nicholson, Peter Fonda, Sandra Bullock and Robert De Niro.

Speaking in 2015, James Horner admitted he hadn't known much about film scoring before working with Corman. His background was in classical music and academia, having studied at the Royal College of Music in London and UCLA, although he had gained some experience working at the American Film Institute, which first sparked his interest: 'I never had any love of film, I never had any desire to be a film composer by any means. I was going to be a serious music composer, and just by accident I was asked to do one of these AFI films and I agreed to do it and fell in love with writing for film.'

Corman's world of low budgets and short deadlines was a learning curve for Horner, who picked up 'the very basic rudiments of film-making and what's expected of you music-wise, and in the course of it, I met Ron Howard who was an editor and also a director, and Jim Cameron who was a cameraman at that point'. Horner's and Cameron's first project together was *Battle Beyond the Stars* in 1980, a sci-fi adventure movie billed as '*The Magnificent Seven* in outer space' – an intriguing bookend in the light of Horner's final score, released posthumously, for the 2016 remake of *The Magnificent Seven*.

Sara Horner, James's widow, also worked at Roger Corman's New World Pictures and spoke to Classic FM in 2017 about her memories of the composer and director at this stage in their careers: 'They were similar in that they were very bright, very creative and very willing to follow their own vision and put it out there. They had a sense of themselves and they knew they were creative. They had strong egos and there seemed to be very little self-doubt in either of them.'

James Cameron, who received his first pay cheque for *Battle Beyond the Stars*, worked on art direction, special photographic effects and miniature design. His first break as writer and director was *The Terminator* in 1984, which topped the American box office for two weeks and opened the door to *Aliens* to him. Horner's big film-scoring break was in another sci-fi realm, for *Star Trek II: The Wrath of Khan* in 1982, which established him as a more mainstream composer. He proved himself capable of following on from Jerry Goldsmith's much-loved music for *Star Trek: The*

*Motion Picture* and created a score which is still highly regarded within the *Star Trek* canon. Horner composed the next film, *Star Trek III: The Search for Spock*, in 1984 and the following year he scored his first movie for Ron Howard, *Cocoon*. By the time *Aliens* came calling, he was mapping out a career that would allow him to compose for a broad cinematic canvas, encompassing thrillers, action, drama, children's movies, romance and sci-fi across the decades.

❦

By all reports, it is unlikely that James Horner would have predicted that **Aliens** would be the first of three successful collaborations with James Cameron. It is well documented that Cameron is a driven director who throws everything into his films and expects the cast and crew to do the same. Combine his passion and temper with a meticulous composer, throw in some serious deadlines, and sparks will inevitably fly.

The sequel to Ridley Scott's 1979 masterpiece – pitched to studios as '*Jaws* in space' – *Aliens* is more of a combat and action movie than out-and-out horror. Widely circulated stories indicate it was a fraught production: Cameron faced hostility from the British crew, who viewed him as an inexperienced substitute for Scott, and refused his entreaties to watch *The Terminator*, which had not yet been released in the UK, by means of proving his worth as writer and director. The biggest threat to the production was time, as Horner recalled: 'Working in the UK was not as speedy as working in the US, and things got bogged down a bit. I was sent over there to ostensibly start writing the score, and they were still editing the movie and had not even looked at the last two reels of the film – and I had sessions booked! I was in this very precarious place of being between Jim, who I had to give space to – I mean, I couldn't ask him for film that wasn't even edited yet – and the studio, who thought he had finished editing and had sent me over to go do the music, to write it.'

Faced with this catch-22, Horner had no choice but to wait and adapt: 'It was a textural film, it was less about themes, so I had to work with footage that wasn't really finished yet. In terms of copying, I had a budget, but I couldn't copy things and send things to the copiers for the orchestra because if the film changed, I'd have to change the music and then we'd have to recopy the parts. What ended up happening was I had to write the whole score in a very few amount of days, which is the sort of famous story about *Aliens*. And it was very intense and very compressed.' Less of a collaboration then, more of a 'just get on with it'. In an interview with America's National Public Radio in 2016, Cameron is aware that he and Horner did not communicate about the music as effectively as they could have: 'There was never really any creative tension, because we never really worked creatively together. That was the problem. *Aliens* was the mistake that we needed to make to know what to do on *Titanic* is really the way I look at it now. It was my first orchestral score. I didn't really know what to expect . . . I didn't know what his process was. He didn't know what my process was – I didn't *have* a process.'

The music for the fight scene between Ripley, played by Sigourney Weaver, and the alien queen was written overnight because Cameron reworked the scene and Horner had to adapt the music to fit. The film itself wasn't completed until the week of release, and Cameron and his editors ended up cutting and splicing sections of Horner's material to fit the finished article. According to Cameron, the composer hadn't given them much choice: 'He did his one-and-a-half day's scoring session at Abbey Road, said, "Here's your music", and then went on to do, I think, *The Name of the Rose.*'

Despite the pressures and frustrations – or possibly in part due to them – Horner delivered an energetic score that's teeming with uncertainty. One highlight is 'Ripley's Rescue', a musical juggernaut with militaristic drums that will grab you, drag you along, make you jump and leave you breathless – all in around three minutes. An additional pressure for the composer was creating a worthy successor to the *Alien* score by Jerry Goldsmith, but the director kept things succinct, nodding to the famous description of the original: 'As Jim said, "It's grunts in space"; grunts are marines and he has this thing for the marines. And that was the brief! Don't think about the artsy stuff, just nail this . . . It was an action film and that was the whole approach from the get-go.'

Horner's nuanced and rich score earned him his first Academy Award nomination. The film received seven Oscar nods in total, winning two, and it was a box-office success with a worldwide gross of around $180 million – nowhere in the league of Cameron's and Horner's next two collaborations but still impressive, especially for an R-rated movie. Despite the accolades, it had been an exhausting and tense project, and it would be safe to assume neither composer nor director was particularly keen to work together again.

Until **Titanic**.

❧

As Cameron recalled, they had both been unhappy with the experience of *Aliens*, 'So when we got back together on *Titanic*, we both bent over so far backwards you could hear vertebrae snapping from a mile away to try to accommodate each other with a process that was going to work creatively as a true collaboration.'

After *Aliens*, Cameron directed *The Abyss* (1989) and *Terminator 2: Judgment Day* (1991), another successful sequel that demonstrated his ability to create box-office gold, becoming the highest-grossing film of

James Horner and James Cameron at the Golden Globe
Awards in 2010, where Cameron won Best Director for *Avatar*.

the year. He followed this up with *True Lies* (1994), his third and final
collaboration with composer Brad Fiedel. Then came his biggest project to date, allowing him to explore his fascination for shipwrecks and
to make the film pitched as '*Romeo and Juliet* on the *Titanic*'. As director, writer and co-producer, Cameron was meticulous in his historical
research and it was the most expensive film ever made at the time, with
an estimated budget of $200 million to reconstruct the RMS *Titanic* and
recreate the sinking of the ship.

In the meantime, Horner had kept up his impressive work rate, at
times scoring in the region of ten films a year, including *Field of Dreams*
(1989), *Patriot Games* (1992) and *Legends of the Fall* (1994). He had

collaborated with Ron Howard again on *Willow* (1988), *Apollo 13* (1995) and *Ransom* (1996), and had begun working with Mel Gibson on *The Man Without a Face* (1993) and *Braveheart* (1995). Cameron had been a fan of the evocative score for *Braveheart*, still one of Horner's most popular and influential works, and listened to that and the score for *Apollo 13* while writing *Titanic*: 'And I thought, "Who am I kidding? It's got to be James. You know, I just gotta figure out how to work with this guy." And so we got together, and it was the most polite meeting you can imagine. But out of it came this sense that: *OK, we kind of screwed up. We got off on the wrong foot. Let's figure out how to fix it.* So we rolled up our sleeves, we figured out how to fix it, and we never looked back.'

The composer describes it as a 'happy coincidence': 'I asked Jim for an interview, and it ends up that I was also on his mind for doing it. He had a couple of people who had approached him and he thought, "That would be a nifty idea but they can't score a movie, they can't do this, they can't do that – what about James?"' They shared a clear vision – at least of what the film should *not* be like – up to a point: 'We didn't want it to be this big Hollywood melodrama,' Horner explained, and Cameron 'told me not to use violins, he told me it's got to be as emotional as it can be, not schmaltzy – he always associates violins with being schmaltzy, although I *did* use violins'.

After this initial conversation, Horner began to work on the score, faced with the particular challenge of composing for a story based on actual events: 'The key to the emotions going through an audience, structurally, as a puzzle for a composer, is suspending or using the knowledge of how the evening ends, how the ship ended, that despite yourself knowing it's not going to end well, you fall in love with the characters ... Whether you like the film or not, it's brilliant film-making on Jim's part to weave a story like that, and the music just marries that, amplifies that, in a way that nothing else can. Despite yourself knowing it's not going to end well, you get sucked in, and then when it doesn't go well, you're completely shattered.'

Horner immersed himself in the film, watching thirty-five hours of raw 'dailies' footage, and according to the director, he created three themes very early on, 'before there was even a cut of the film. He played them for me on piano and they were so emotional, they were so heart-breaking – just in a simple solo piano form – that I knew we had a great score, from that moment on . . . And that was just right off the bat, with zero input from me, other than James reacting to the footage that I had shot.' Some of Horner's early piano sketches featured in the final score, such as the scene in which Jack draws a picture of Rose. Apparently the composer offered to orchestrate it or get a more skilled pianist to record it, but the director convinced him he'd captured the essence of the scene.

While the composing process was far more harmonious than their earlier collaboration, the production for *Titanic* was, as with *Aliens*, beset with crises, mostly related to time and budgetary restraints. Their com-parative closeness is evident in how they communicated with each other during the making of *Titanic*, however, and the composer seems to have become an ally for the director: 'We got to a point where he had delayed the release of the film several times, he had just given up his salary – he's very honourable that way – he felt he had completely screwed up the studio and he just wanted to make the best film possible. The effects were dribbling in, he was doing the editing – he had four editors but he would edit at night himself because "Nobody else got it" . . . We had this discussion about the success of the movie and I told him, "You're in the best possible position because the world thinks it's going to be a complete screw-up and disaster, and we know how stunning it is. It's the best! It'll be such a shock to an audience to finally see it and have them so moved."'

Cameron has said he got to know Horner – as a person and as a talent – when working on *Titanic*, as he told National Public Radio (NPR): 'I think the depth of his emotion and his sensitivity is what gave him a lot of his musical talent. I mean, sure, he was classically trained and he was a pianist and he knew what he was doing technically, but I think it was that he, himself, was a very emotional person. And I think that was a big part of what he brought to the table as a composer.'

A solid example of a film score created from a communicated and shared vision between composer and director, *Titanic* is not only the highest-selling primarily orchestral soundtrack ever, but it's one of the best-selling albums of all time, remaining at the top of the Billboard chart for a record-breaking sixteen weeks. In retrospect, did the composer anticipate its incredible success? 'I had no idea it would do anything like what it did. I just knew that there were no worries that this wasn't going to play. I said it's too good a movie, and if it works on me, I know it'll work on an audience. We discussed it a few times, and history proved that right.'

The popularity of Horner's score is evident to this day, and in August 2017 it was revealed as number 1 in the Ultimate Classic FM Chart, making it the best-selling classical and orchestral album of the past quarter-century. His widow, Sara, was asked what she thought his response to this accolade would be: 'He was a very individualistic thinker so I don't know if he would feel like that was his best work, but certainly the public love it. What I would say is – and I think this is true for all the composers I know – is that their relationship with the audience was where they felt most emotionally connected in the world. I think touching the inner feeling world of the audience was what composers most wish to do, and when he was successful at doing that, I think James felt like he had fulfilled his destiny. Really reaching out to people because he was socially really shy, a lot of composers are, and the deep, intimate contact they have with people is through their work.'

*Titanic* broke box-office records and picked up fourteen Academy Award nominations, winning eleven, a feat matched by *Ben-Hur* and, later, *The Lord of the Rings: Return of the King*. James Horner collected two of them, for Best Original Score and, along with lyricist Will Jennings, Best Original Song. He alluded to the story behind 'My Heart Will Go On' in his acceptance speech: after thanking singer Céline Dion and her husband and manager René Angélil, James credited 'Jim Cameron, for being in a good mood that day when I brought you the song'. A brief but fascinating glimpse into their partnership. The director had not wanted a song over the closing credits, but Horner believed otherwise, so composed a song, recorded a demo with Dion, and presented it to Cameron who, as it would seem, was not averse to negotiation that day. The rest is chart history, and yet another reason to secure *Titanic*'s place in popular culture.

≈

Before turning to Horner's and Cameron's third and final collaboration, *Avatar*, it is worth finding out more about the composer's approach to film scoring by exploring his work with Ron Howard. The former actor, better known to many as Richie Cunningham from *Happy Days*, has a reputation for being one of the nicest guys in Hollywood. Horner scored seven films for him in total, starting with *Cocoon* in 1985 and most recently *The Missing* in 2003, and the director shared his experiences of working with the composer, and of hearing the news about his death, in 2016: 'It had been some years since we'd worked together. I always feel that, movie by movie, it's important to cast the composer the way you would your lead actor, and so just as I've worked with Tom Hanks five times, there are certain people that I enjoy collaborating with. James was one of those.'

The collaboration could have actually begun earlier, because Horner was asked to score the 1984 mermaid romcom *Splash*. Displaying an integrity that not many would have shown at the start of their careers, when presumably the temptation is just to take a job, any job, for the money and experience, he admitted, 'I didn't think I was the right guy. I thought I was miscast, and I didn't want to screw up my first job with them. And I told them. I was hoping that they wouldn't fall in love with whoever did that score, that they would then bond with that person, so I was risking that.' It paid off, because the eventual composer, Lee Holdridge, didn't deliver the goods to a sufficient extent to erode Howard's esteem for Horner, and the composer signed up for *Cocoon* the following year.

There seems to have been a real sense of truth and integrity to all of Horner's decisions as a film composer. A notable cinematic 'what might have been' is when he declined the offer of scoring the *Lord of the Rings* films because he couldn't spend the required time in New Zealand due to family commitments. Later in his career, he offered to score 2015 boxing drama *Southpaw* for free because he loved the father–daughter relationship at the centre of the film.

The search for the truth – the core – of the story was a binding force for Howard and Horner, and the composer observed their shared motivations in that Ron 'has this heart which comes through on a lot of his films, and that's what I go for, that's what I aim for on every project. I never aim for the surface elements. In all the films I work on, there's always that "What is the heart of the film?" – and I try and nail that. And Ron is so warm-hearted, it just happened, we just clicked like that.'

Howard has described Horner as 'a great artist and a wonderful storyteller' who also taught him, directly or indirectly, about the impact of music on a movie: 'We were exactly the same age, so we kind of grew up together, advancing our careers at a similar pace, and James was really the composer who helped me to understand how the performances and the camera decisions, the camera movements, could influence a composer and what a great storyteller a movie composer can be. It's about reinforcing nuances, ideas that literal language can't quite convey. The camerawork almost gets it there but the music completes the telling of that story, of that moment.' And there are so many examples of this from their collaborations: 'The Launch' from *Apollo 13* and 'A Kaleidoscope of Mathematics' from *A Beautiful Mind* are great places to start.

Despite collaborating more frequently with Hans Zimmer in the decade leading up to Horner's death, Howard admits, 'I really miss James, and I was always, always, in the back of my mind assuming we'd work together again. In fact, I had a great lunch with him a couple of months before he died, and it was terrific to reconnect with him. It wasn't about a particular project ... he was very busy, working on a lot of different movies, but he had really fallen in love with flying. People don't realise what an avid hobbyist James was. He could make radio-controlled helicopters from scratch and fly them! He had really fallen in love with flying, and that crash was devastating for me but I knew from our last conversation that he was doing something that he truly loved.'

≈

Back to Cameron and Horner for their third and final collaboration. If anyone thought they might sit back and rest on their laurels after *Titanic*, or go for something on a smaller scale, they were much mistaken. Cameron had actually written a treatment for *Avatar* in 1994, with plans to start making it after *Titanic*, but the intended 1999 release came and went because, according to the director, the technology wasn't developed enough. He was willing to wait another decade to ensure his vision of the planet Pandora and its blue natives, the Na'vi, was realised to its fullest potential – and, yet again, the risk paid off. Not only was the film praised for its groundbreaking visual effects, but from an estimated budget of over $300 million, it went on to earn more than $2 billion worldwide.

The composer spent over two years scoring *Avatar* and, unusually for him, considering his work rate in the 1980s and 1990s, he didn't take on any other projects during this time. When asked about the long gestation period for both film and score, the composer said that Cameron 'wanted a big commitment. He ended up not dealing with music for quite a while, but the whole brief for me was that it had to be emotional but the music had to be of a sound world that transcended stuff I'd done before [and] had to match the brilliance of his visuals.'

For the director, it was a no-brainer to recruit Horner for the project because 'we had established a good working rapport, and I think that's really the most important thing. It's like having a tango partner – you've got to have absolute trust.' The composer completely understood, and could cope with, the pressures facing him: 'I couldn't be even a millimetre less. I had to be right where his visuals were, if not better.' Horner might have even enjoyed being pushed to his creative limits, knowing by this time that that's what the director would expect from him. He worked with an ethnomusologist and recorded sections with a chorus singing the constructed Na'vi language. In fact, he described the music as two scores merged into one, as the Na'vi music combines with a more human, or traditional, sound world – and that took a lot of preparation: 'I wanted the music to be as stunning sonically as the visuals were, and I couldn't get away with just playing it on the piano, I had to mock it all up and that takes time.' Sara Horner remembers that, during this process, her husband 'would record and then they would make something else, and there were constant changes because at that point it's much more process-oriented. There were mock-ups being made every day, and then Jim listens to them and comments on them so he could participate much more in the process, and they were both perfectionists, so James was just exhausted!'

In a way, it's not surprising that there was no musical 'eureka' moment with the *Avatar* score, as Cameron described with *Titanic*. Creating music for a planet set in the future involved a fair amount of back and forth: the composer would share extracts with the director, 'and he would reject some of them because he thought he had heard them before, he'd reject some of them for being too dissonant, he'd reject some of them for various other reasons, and then he would accept, and accept, and accept, reject, accept, accept, accept – and slowly we wove our way through putting the score together. In addition to which, the film was constantly changing, until release practically.'

So, elements of the making of *Aliens*, then, but this time countered with over two decades of experience in the film industry and more of a shared understanding between the composer and director. Areas of potential conflict still cropped up, and Horner felt the need to confront Cameron on occasion, to ensure the heart of the movie could shine through: 'I thought it was too effects-driven and I was worried he had nudged it slightly in favour of being a fan-boy movie. I thought he should just edge back a tiny bit. It was just us . . . at a watch-through screening, doing the dubbing, and he agreed. And we . . . took out the music he had earlier rejected and put it back – and it just was enough to warm it slightly and not make it quite as sterile.'

Horner was modest about this input – 'I don't know if it would have made any difference, any more emotional than that or less emotional' – but by offering his perspective, he served as a reminder to Cameron to focus on the heart of the story. The composer was well aware of how far the two had come in order to have such an open discussion: 'He thinks very intensely about everything he does and that's the level we exchange at. He trusts my instincts – and the fact that I would say that meant a lot.'

The *Avatar* score has Horner's trademark sweeping motifs and use of native instruments, and there are occasional nods to Ennio Morricone's music for *The Mission*. A stand-out cue, 'The Bioluminescence of the Night', features pipes and chimes to enchanting effect, and it seems to light up the world around you when you listen to it. Elsewhere, the choir and dogged brass fanfares build the scale of threat and danger during 'War', for the clash between the Na'vi and humans on Pandora. When asked if Horner was happy with the final score, Sara said she felt both men were, describing them as 'the kind of people that are willing to die for their art! Honestly, they'll drive themselves, and the people around them, as hard and as far as they can.'

Nominated for nine Academy Awards in 2010, including Best Picture and Best Director – both losing to Kathryn Bigelow's *The Hurt Locker* – *Avatar* won three Oscars for Best Cinematography, Best Art Direction and Best Visual Effects. Horner was in the running for Best Original Score, his tenth and final nomination, and it is somehow fitting that at this ceremony the Academy gave an honorary award to Roger Corman 'for his rich engendering of films and film-makers'.

❧

A director with near-limitless ambition, James Cameron plans to release four *Avatar* sequels: the first is due for release in December 2020. Horner had been about to start work on the follow-up at the end of 2015, and while we'll never know how he would have extended this musical universe, there is some solace in the director and composer being able to reach a creative understanding. As Cameron acknowledges, 'I will miss the collaboration, I will miss the fun, I will miss the creation. You know, certainly miss him as a person. He only lived just over the hill from me, a couple miles away, and he'd pop back and forth to my place and me to his when we were working together. I'm not saying we hung out and played video games the whole time in between movies – it wasn't like that. But, I'm going to miss him as a human being first, I'm going to miss him as a collaborator, just because it was good, and we knew what to do, and we knew how to talk to each other.'

Speaking about the role of the composer within the film-making process, Horner shared a typically instinctive perspective about the importance of communication: 'It's always been important to me how I get along with people, but now it's even more important that they know who I am and that we really click . . . before I agree to do a film. I've seen a lot of films where I've been asked to do them, and I just know I'll never get along with the director, I just know he's not into the same aesthetic I am.'

Having decades of experience with so many other directors no doubt allowed Horner to value certain individuals' personalities and working methods but also to recognise his own worth. As he explained, 'The composer is part of the nuclear family. There's the producer, the director, the writer perhaps, the studio, of course, but they're kept away until the film's ready to be seen – and there's the composer. So you're part of a very intimate relationship, and my responsibility is to just make it perfect.'

Perfection – striving to create the best story and tell it in the best way possible – lay at the core of the Horner–Cameron collaboration. Despite conflict, they helped to push each other further, and grew to recognise their individual strengths and flaws. They might not have compromised, but they adapted. As Horner observed, 'Jim's wired like me, he's a perfectionist. I do get along very well with him despite the difficulty of working with him. He has different people skills than I do! But he puts 1,000 per cent of himself into something, while a lot of other people bail out somewhere in that process, and that's part of Jim's mystique.'

##  Collaboration History

*Battle Beyond the Stars* (1980), production design and special effects by Cameron

*Aliens* (1986), written and directed by Cameron

*Titanic* (1997), written, directed, co-produced and co-edited by Cameron

*Avatar* (2009), written, directed, co-produced and co-edited by Cameron

##  Suggested Playlist

*Battle Beyond the Stars*, Main Title

*Aliens*, Ripley's Rescue

*Aliens*, Bishop's Countdown

*Aliens*, Resolution and Hyperspace

*Titanic*, Rose

*Titanic*, Southampton

*Titanic*, An Ocean of Memories

*Avatar*, The Bioluminescence of the Night

*Avatar*, Jake's First Flight

*Avatar*, War

# 7

# MAURICE JARRE
# AND DAVID LEAN

*'Ah, then it's a gift.'*

Collaborating on just four films over three decades, Sir David Lean and Maurice Jarre nonetheless made cinematic history. From the staggering success of *Lawrence of Arabia* to Lean's final film, *A Passage to India*, Jarre provided the epic, sweeping music to match Lean's landscapes on-screen, from the eastern deserts and snowy Russian forests to the stormy Irish coastline and sweltering Indian cities. Between them they created some of the most popular and enduring works for cinema.

David Lean remains one of the UK's most respected directors, with a reputation for his dedicated and exacting approach to film-making. He directed sixteen feature films in a career spanning forty years, and remains the only Brit to win the Academy Award for Best Director on more than one occasion. In 1999, the British Film Institute compiled a list of the top 100 British films, and Lean had an impressive three in the top 10 alone: *Brief Encounter* at 2, *Lawrence of Arabia* at 3, and *Great Expectations* at 5. With a background as a successful film editor, Lean had a fine eye and ear for the pacing of storytelling, and in 1962 when he first met the young French composer nearly two decades his junior, he quickly understood that this inventive musician could capture the emotion at the heart of the story. Jarre created memorable scores, inseparable from Lean's films, and won the Oscar for Best Original Score for three of them. Put simply, the director knew what he wanted from the music, and the composer delivered the perfect atmospheric and dramatic sounds for his vision.

⁂

Born in 1924 in Lyon, Maurice Jarre quit his college studies in engineering to enrol at the prestigious Paris Conservatoire. He studied percussion and worked as a timpanist, and later credited this role with providing an informative musical education, giving him the perfect perspective from which to observe the makings and machinations of the orchestra. As part of his course, he had to study the music of five different cultures and he chose Russian, Indian, Japanese, South American and Arabic styles, which would come in very useful later when composing film scores for exotic locations. After graduating, he played in the orchestra of a theatre company in Paris, where he was also the arranger and conductor, and in 1951 he became the composer for the Théâtre National Populaire in Lyon, writing original scores for a variety of plays including *Richard II* and *Macbeth*. He would spend twelve years as music director there, but started composing for film the following year, with a score for an anti-war documentary short directed by the French film-maker Georges Franju. This was the start of a partnership between Jarre and Franju that would include two more short films and five feature films.

His early working relationship with Franju gave Jarre an understanding of the skills required for a successful collaboration, as well as allowing him to develop what was already a unique and recognisable style as a film composer. Throughout his career, he pulled off the tricky task of composing music that was recognisably his, yet he was never pigeonholed by it. In the early 1960s, however, while his career was on the up in France, he needed to work on a British or American movie if he wanted to step into the international arena.

⇌

From Paris and Lyon we turn to Croydon, where David Lean was born in 1908. A fairly unremarkable pupil – his school reports offer little suggestion of future job prospects – a gift from his uncle set him on his career path. When he was ten, he received a Brownie box camera, and in a 1985 television documentary, *David Lean: A Life in Film*, he told Melvyn Bragg that this present was 'the biggest compliment I'd ever been paid'.

When he was allowed to go to the cinema as a teenager, he fell in love with film. On leaving school, he managed a year as a clerk at his father's firm before announcing he wanted to work in cinema, so his dad arranged a meeting with a fellow accountant at the Gaumont-British Picture Corporation. The young Lean was paid £1 a week to do all sorts of jobs at the Lime Grove Studios, from lugging cameras around and making the tea to a short stint as wardrobe mistress, before entering the cutting room. Developing editing skills when working on newsreels, he learned about the practicalities of film-making, such as working to tight deadlines and applying imaginative techniques within creative constraints, and he rose up the ranks. By 1941, when he edited Powell and Pressburger's *49th Parallel*, he was a highly respected film editor.

Lean had Noël Coward to thank for his entry into the world of directing. Coward was looking for a good technician to co-direct with him on *In Which We Serve* (1942) and several people recommended Lean. The original plan was for him to focus on the technical aspects while Coward concentrated on his fellow actors, but as Lean gratefully reflected, 'Noël got bored very quickly', so he took over all of the directorial responsibilities. He went on to adapt several of Coward's plays into films including *Brief Encounter* (1945), for which he earned the first of seven Academy Award nominations for Best Director.

Even at this stage, Lean's meticulous approach to film-making was well known. The director Ronald Neame, who worked as his producer, described how he would obsess over every word in the script. They worked together on the Charles Dickens adaptations *Oliver Twist* and *Great Expectations*, and Lean became heavily involved with the screenplay, editing and cinematography as well as directing. He gained a reputation for creating memorable scenes with little or no dialogue, suggesting a real grasp of the power of sound within a film, be that speech or music. During the 1940s and 1950s he worked with some of Britain's finest composers, such as Richard Addinsell on *Blithe Spirit* (1945) and *The Passionate Friends* (1949), and Malcolm Arnold on *The Sound Barrier* (1952), *Hobson's Choice* (1954), and his biggest hit before *Lawrence of Arabia*, the British-American co-production *The Bridge on the River Kwai*.

Lean's genius at creating visual masterpieces was given a new lease of life in 1955 when he started working in Venice on *Summertime*, released in the UK as *Summer Madness*. From then on, all of his films were set and shot abroad. His projects became larger in scale as the 1950s progressed, and *The Bridge on the River Kwai* displayed his breadth of vision. The highest-grossing movie of 1957, this epic war film about British soldiers in a Japanese prison camp in Burma was garlanded with seven Oscars, including Best Picture and Best Director.

❦

After the success of *The Bridge on the River Kwai*, David Lean and producer Sam Spiegel were keen to work together again. They initially planned to make a film about Mahatma Gandhi, but the project was abandoned. Then, the film rights to T. E. Lawrence's book *The Seven Pillars of Wisdom* became available and Spiegel snapped them up. Lawrence was the illegitimate son of an Irish baronet, and was considered a rather romantic figure, depicted in the film as uniting Bedouin peoples of the Arab peninsula to fight in the First World War and then to push for independence. Various biopics had been in the pipeline but they hadn't come to fruition and this was a story Lean wanted to tell, exploring wider themes of identity and divided allegiance.

All in all, ***Lawrence of Arabia*** (1962) took nearly three years to make: after extensive preparation and location work by Lean, filming began in May 1961 in the Jordan desert known as Jebel Tubeiq, near the Saudi Arabian border. Film shoots in Spain, Morocco and England followed, and a royal premiere was set for 9 December 1962. As the project entered its post-production phase, David Lean and Sam Spiegel turned to the matter of the composer.

Here's how Maurice Jarre got his big career break. At first, the director had assumed that Malcolm Arnold would score it, following on from their earlier collaborations and the composer's Oscar win for *The Bridge on the River Kwai*. The producer, ever mindful of appealing to as broad an audience as possible, wanted to commission both Arnold and William Walton, so the prestigious list of associates could feature two leading British composers. He asked the editor Anne V. Coates to provide a two-hour rough cut for them to watch, and they are said to have arrived at the screening room after a long liquid lunch. After giggling – and snoozing – throughout, the two composers didn't hold back in their criticism, with Arnold describing it as 'terrible'. Once Lean and Spiegel heard the feedback, that was the end of that.

Another early plan was for the score to be in two parts, to demonstrate the British forces and the eastern setting, so Benjamin Britten was brought on board to write the former and Aram Khachaturian the latter. Jarre, whose recent work on the French film *Sundays and Cybele*, a project Spiegel had been involved in financially, had impressed the producer and director, was invited to fill in the gaps. Jarre was delighted to be part of this trio and in July 1962 he spent time in London researching T. E. Lawrence. The following month he discovered the collaboration had been cancelled: Khachaturian couldn't leave Russia and Britten had requested a year and a half to compose his part of the score due to other work commitments. With four months to go before the premiere, that wasn't an option.

Sam Spiegel's next plan was for Richard Rodgers to step into the frame. Hard to believe now that the man behind *The Sound of Music* might have scored *Lawrence of Arabia*, but the producer thought the Broadway composer would be a good fit, having penned the 'oriental' musical *The King and I* and a Second World War television documentary *Victory at Sea*. In September, Spiegel returned from the States to inform Jarre that Rodgers would write 90 per cent of the score, and he would orchestrate it and provide the remaining 10 per cent. Jarre wasn't best pleased, as he had already turned down film-scoring work back in France, but accepted the new arrangement and asked whether the new composer would come to London, or whether he should go to America to meet him. Spiegel didn't think that would be necessary, stating that Rodgers would stay in New York and send over his themes in a few weeks. During September, while Rodgers used Robert Bolt's screenplay as his primary inspiration, Jarre watched as much film footage as he could – over forty hours' worth, all told. Initially he didn't watch scenes with the main actors, Peter O'Toole and Omar Sharif, but rather visuals of the desert, and musical ideas began to take shape in his mind.

Later that month, Spiegel received Rodgers' themes by mail and arranged for a pianist to play them to him, Lean and Jarre. The 'Oriental Theme' was not particularly impressive – Jarre later said it sounded like 'something left over from *The King and I*' – and the 'Love Theme' wasn't much better. The third theme was a British military number, and the pianist is said to have commented that it was an old march, not an original, by which time Lean's patience had been well and truly tested. After a frustrated outburst at his producer – 'Sam, what is all this rubbish? I am supposed to be editing the film, and you take up my time with the nonsense!' – he then asked Jarre if he had composed anything. Jarre played a piece simply called 'The Theme from *Lawrence of Arabia*', and he recalled that Lean put his hand on his shoulder and announced, 'Sam, this chap has got the theme. Maurice, *you* are going to do it!'

And so began six weeks of writing and recording two hours of music, scored for a hundred instruments. A daunting challenge, and one that Jarre apparently completed by dramatically limiting his sleep – one story claims he got through it by working for four hours at a time followed by a ten-minute nap on his office couch – but he was prepared, having immersed himself in the footage and the story. He was already transfixed by the images of the desert so the themes came naturally to him.

From the grand opening timpani to the percussive crashes and brass fanfare, followed by *those* strings, the scale, romance and pure hummability of the 'Overture' instantly transport the audience to the heat of the desert. Maurice Jarre was keen to include a range of instruments to capture the spirit of the location, including a rather eerie-sounding type of electric keyboard called an ondes martenot. Now synonymous with the sweltering desert heat, it's hard to listen to the score without picturing the landscape or the famous scene in which Lawrence blows out a match and then the audience feasts on a sunrise filling the screen. The composer, who described the visual imagery in this editing cut as poetry, accentuated this glorious moment with his music, but it's interesting to note he exercised restraint in other key scenes. When Sherif Ali, played by Omar Sharif, is introduced emerging from the mirage on the far horizon, riding a camel, there is no music. He is a dot on the landscape, gradually becoming bigger as he approaches Lawrence and his guide, Tafas, but the only sound we hear are the camel's footsteps on the sand, allowing the audience's curiosity about this new character to build.

Finally, *Lawrence of Arabia* was complete in time for the London premiere. The film came to 222 minutes and was shown with an intermission, but later it was cut by twenty minutes, at Spiegel's request. Another fifteen minutes were later deleted on reissues, but a director's cut was released in 1989, with some additional musical cues – 'First Entrance to the Desert', 'Night and Star', 'Lawrence and Tafas' – that beautifully demonstrate further experimentation with the famous theme. Later, in 2000, it was restored for a special DVD release, and directors Steven Spielberg and Martin Scorsese were involved in the project because it had been so influential to them. Spielberg has said this was the first film he saw that made him want to become a film-maker.

*Lawrence of Arabia* received ten Academy Award nominations and won seven, including Best Original Score, Best Picture, Best Director, Best Film Editing and Best Cinematography for Freddie Young, another regular Lean collaborator. The director said in the early 1980s that the

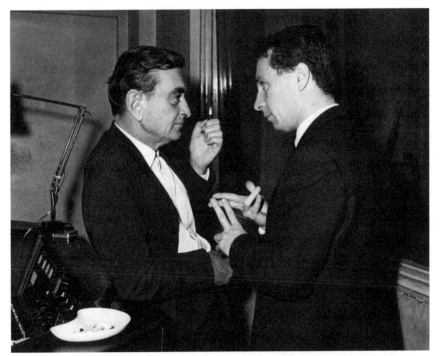

David Lean and Maurice Jarre in 1963, when they
were working on *Lawrence of Arabia*.

making of this film had been one of the best experiences of his life. Lean
had a reputation for being demanding with his close crew members and
somewhat dismissive of actors – Omar Sharif once said he found it easy
to hate him because he treated people on set like objects – but a clear
bond had formed between director and composer.

≈

Although an exacting director, David Lean was loyal and willing to take
a stand to ensure he had the best people on his team, and he insisted that
Maurice Jarre worked on his next project, ***Doctor Zhivago*** (1965), an
adaptation of Boris Pasternak's Nobel Prize-winning novel. The MGM
music department acknowledged the composer's skill at scoring for the

desert landscapes, but thought they could get someone better for the snowy Russian setting of this film. Lean did not agree. The studio, who were looking for a hit after a series of financial failures, yielded to him, and he recruited many other *Lawrence of Arabia* collaborators, including screenwriter Robert Bolt, costume designer Phyllis Dalton and production designer John Box.

The director wanted to make a more romance-driven film, and the love story between Lara and Yuri set during the Russian Revolution seemed just right. The book was banned in the Soviet Union, so Lean had to turn elsewhere for filming and, following his experiences shooting scenes for *Lawrence of Arabia*, decided on Spain. Some of the winter scenes were filmed in Finland but for the most part the task was to turn Spain into Russia, which was all the more challenging during an unseasonably warm winter. Thousands of tonnes of crushed white marble dust were used to create a snow effect in a forest as they brought Moscow to the outskirts of Madrid.

*Doctor Zhivago* is another visual triumph, packed full of memorable scenes, and was promoted as MGM's successor to *Gone with the Wind*. Keen to make the most of this incipient hit, the studio wanted to release the film in time to be eligible for the Academy Awards, as well as opening in cinemas before Christmas to attract audiences during the holidays. Filming finished on 7 October 1965, so Lean had just over two months to do the editing, an enormous pressure considering he usually took around six months to complete that complex task. For the composer, however, this was a luxury compared with the deadline pressure of *Lawrence of Arabia*. Perhaps he would be able to sleep for a whole hour at a time!

Since Jarre's Oscar win, he had scored more international films, such as *The Longest Day* (1963) and *Behold a Pale Horse* (1964) and he made his first trip to Hollywood in 1965 to work on *The Collector*. He recalled the director briefing him thoroughly for *Doctor Zhivago*, in keeping with his meticulous approach to all aspects of the film-making process. Lean once revealed, 'I think a composer must be told what to do. Very often the music supplies half the emotional and dramatic effect. Seeing a film before the music is added, an observer might think, "Well, that shot's completely unnecessary." But with the music he will see the reason for it. I think that to have the composer on the set before the film is finished is generally a waste of time. With Maurice Jarre I wait until I get a rough cut. Then I show it to him and discuss, very broadly, where music is probably to be used, and what it should do.'

Lean couldn't read or write a word of music, but over the decades as a director, he grew in confidence when it came to telling a composer exactly what he wanted. He was always rigidly loyal to the script – so much so that he would often dictate the intonation to the actors, much to their annoyance. Whenever words failed him, he would invite actors to look through the camera so they could understand his point of view. When it came to the music, he could not be specific in his instructions, and could say only, 'Well, Maurice, I think you can do better', which was precisely his reaction to Jarre's first attempt at a love theme for *Doctor Zhivago*. Three of the composer's themes were rejected by the director. Sensing Jarre's disappointment, Lean had a brainwave: take a break.

The director told the composer to spend the weekend with his girl-friend in the mountains of Los Angeles, with the hope that he would find inspiration. Lean reminded Jarre that the theme did not need to be specifically Russian in tone, but rather a universal theme of love, and it's said the composer had such a good weekend that he sat down at his piano on the Monday morning and wrote 'Lara's Theme' in one hour. On the film's release, some critics felt it was over-used in the film, but Lean and producer Carlo Ponti were so taken with the theme that they couldn't resist using it at every opportunity, and the director attributed the success of *Doctor Zhivago* in part to this piece of music. With the addition of lyrics by Paul Francis Webster, it was transformed into 'Somewhere My Love' and was a huge hit in the singles charts, pleasing the studio no end by bringing awareness of the film to a wider audience.

Jarre had been inspired by the great Russian composers, such as Tchaikovsky and Rimsky-Korsakov, for this score. The scale of the film required a big sound and the composer worked with a 110-piece orchestra, a 40-member chorus and a group of balalaika players. He incorporated the recently invented Moog synthesiser into the score but the balalaika, a Russian stringed instrument with a triangular body, produces an idiosyncratic, vibrant sound. It stands out, not least because of its significance in the story. Lieutenant General Yevgraf Andreyevich Zhivago believes a young woman called Tanya may be the child of Lara and his half-brother Yuri, and when he learns that she is self-taught on the very instrument that Lara played so well, he responds knowingly, 'Ah, then it's a gift.' No one in the MGM studio orchestra could play the balalaika, but that didn't deter the composer, who went to a Russian Orthodox church in downtown Los Angeles to recruit a group of people who could. Jarre later revealed that they were unable to read music, so he taught them sixteen bars which they learned by heart.

The score for *Doctor Zhivago* serves as an aural description of some of the scenes in the film, such as the burial of Yuri's mother, with the music accompanying the dirt hitting the coffin in 'Funeral Song'. The composer reinforced the sound effect with zither, tubular bells and kettledrums to enhance the impact, and make it feel more shocking to the viewer. While Jarre was working on these detailed elements, Lean was busy in the cutting room. He was still putting the finishing touches to the edit when Jarre finished recording the score with the MGM orchestra on 14 December 1965, just eight days before the premiere.

At over three hours, *Doctor Zhivago* was another long slice of Lean and not all the critics were favourably disposed towards it, owing to its romanticised representation of the Russian Revolution. The director didn't always have the best of relationships with critics, but what did that matter? The audiences loved *Doctor Zhivago*. The film was Lean's greatest box-office success and remains one of the highest-grossing films of all time, when the figures are adjusted for inflation. Winning five Oscars from a total of ten nominations, it was lauded for its screenplay, costume design, art direction, cinematography and, of course, its score.

≈

Another David Lean film, another evocative setting; this time the west coast of Ireland, although here the director's successful streak came to a halt. **Ryan's Daughter** (1970) is a retelling of *Madame Bovary* by Gustave Flaubert. Described on promotional material as 'a story of love', it concerns a young, married Irish woman who has an affair with a British soldier in a remote village after the Easter Rising of 1916. This was Jarre's favourite among Lean's films, and his preferred score from their collaboration. The director specifically asked the composer not to write typically Irish music, and while some folk music and jigs are incorporated, the overall effect is tender and wistful, a contrast to the sweeping scale of their earlier projects. Both Lean and Jarre felt that big orchestrations were not fitting for this tale, and 'Rosy's Theme', starting with a simple flute melody, feels lighter in comparison to the music for Lara and Lawrence.

In keeping with their previous collaborations – and in contrast to most of the other partnerships in this book – the composer was not involved at the start of the film or invited to visit the set. During a radio interview in 1970 to promote *Ryan's Daughter*, Lean explained how the score was created after Jarre had watched the early cut of the film: 'He will write some main themes. He doesn't attempt to fit it to the picture at all. He just plays it on the piano. And it's frightfully difficult to tell, because he'll say, "Well, bum-bum-bum . . . this will be the violins; this will be the drums; and then there'll be a very sad solo horn, I hope, coming in here." And so on and so forth. And then when one's got the picture finally cut and you're not going to make any more alterations, you decide exactly where the music's going.' Lean would then provide Jarre with precise duration requirements for the cues, and the composer would work watching the scenes on a small movie projector called a moviola, playing the piano along to what he saw, sometimes recording what he played onto a tape-recorder so he could then assess how, and whether, it fitted with the picture.

After the initial, detailed briefing discussions between the director and the composer, and the early themes played on the piano, Lean would leave Jarre to compose and orchestrate the full score, but would return to provide more input during the recording session which, in a pre-digital age with no tools at their disposal to create mock-ups of scenes or the score, he described as an 'absolute nightmare': 'There are anything up to a hundred musicians sitting there – and you literally hear the thing as it's meant to be for the first time. And every now and again I'll ask him to do a slight adjustment. I'll say, "This has an overall gay feeling to it. Can you put in a touch of sadness somewhere?" Or, "Can you make it a little more exciting there?" It's very hard to describe.'

Jarre's one big bold moment in his comparatively muted score comes during the crucial storm scene, the reason the production took twelve months instead of the expected six, because the director was waiting for (literally) the perfect storm. The composer throws in big percussion, brass and woodwind to accompany the characters as they are bashed about by the elements as they try to recover a shipment of arms from the sea, and the unleashed instrumentation adds to the drama. For a director who was so skilled at editing, and piecing the film together, the placement of music was a crucial consideration. As Lean explained during the making of *A Passage to India*, 'I get a tremendous kick out of seeing a sequence cut, I'm in the middle of it now, putting music to a film, getting the dialogue balance right, I find it immensely exciting.'

One of the highest-grossing films of 1970, *Ryan's Daughter* received four Academy Award nominations, winning for Best Cinematography and Best Supporting Actor. Not a real failure by any means, but it pales in comparison with the other runaway successes of the Jarre–Lean collaboration. Later praised for its depiction of the Irish coastline and the claustrophobia of rural village life, at the time of release the critics had their knives out. David Lean met up with the National Society of Film Critics in New York to discuss their unfavourable reviews, and was shocked at the vehemently negative reaction. After spending hours being told everything that was wrong with *Ryan's Daughter*, he decided to take a break from directing.

At the time, he was so shaken he claimed he would never make another film, though he did direct a documentary for New Zealand television about the salvaging of an anchor from one of Captain Cook's ships. He also planned an epic two-part dramatisation of the *Bounty* mutiny story with his regular collaborator Robert Bolt, but Lean left the project after Bolt had a stroke and could no longer complete the screenplay because he felt the writer's inclusion was vital to the film's success. It was fourteen years before Lean directed another feature-length film, and it would be his last.

David Lean's sixteenth film, *A Passage to India* (1984), was an adaptation of the popular E. M. Forster novel, set against the backdrop of the British Raj. Lean had been interested in making the film after seeing the theatrical version in 1960, but the author did not grant him permission. When Forster died in 1970, the governing board of fellows at King's College Cambridge inherited the rights to his books, and these became available to film-makers a decade later when a professor who was a film enthusiast became the chief executor. Lord Brabourne, who had produced Franco Zeffirelli's acclaimed *Romeo and Juliet*, bought the film rights with the intention of producing it, and was keen for Lean to direct, as a great admirer of his work. The contract for the rights stipulated that Santha Rama Rau, who had adapted the book for the theatre, would write the screenplay, but her initial efforts were rejected by the director and producer, so Lean worked on the script himself. Back to his usual ways of working, the film was shot entirely on location, and the fictional town of Chandrapore was rebuilt in the grounds of a maharaja's palace in Bangalore.

Jarre described the director as being rejuvenated by this project, indicating that the hiatus in film-making had been a difficult time for Lean, as well it might for someone who lived and breathed cinema. Everything had been visualised by him in the script, including the use of music and where it should start and stop. In an interview in 1989, two years before his death, he describes a more collaborative way of working with the composer, despite his customary clear orders: 'I always participate in the writing of the screenplay, and I always give directions for the music. When it should begin, when it stops, what it should express. When the composer starts getting involved – you'd think I was married to Maurice Jarre – I show him the script. I talk with him, I tell him the mood of the movie, and very often I'll call upon him to rescue me because I've messed it all up.' An interesting admission from someone who had such a clear vision for the film, and a touching insight of the trust between director and composer. Lean continues, 'He'll ask why, and then I tell him, "Here we need to have a dramatic feeling and it's simply not there. You can do it with the music." People always think that doing a movie is like writing a book. All it takes is to sit down in front of a blank page and that you have all the time in the world. As a director, my problem is that I constantly hear the sound of dollar bills flying off. You have to work very, very quickly, and you can make huge mistakes. Or you might forget things. Music helps fix those lapses.'

Jarre, who once described Lean as 'very demanding' but clearly respected the director's film-making vision, was undoubtedly bolstered by Lean's continued trust in his abilities. The composer may well have relished yet another musical challenge that would allow him to experiment with more instruments, including the sitar and theremin alongside the trusted ondes martenot. The title music starts eerily before settling into an assured, jolly rhythm, but Lean instructed Jarre to compose more romantic, sensual cues for the scenes of Adela Quested's self-discovery, such as the bicycle ride that leads her to a garden of erotic statues. The music was required to portray the emotions that the repressed British woman would not be able to articulate, and these were vital for the story, in which she would accuse a young Indian doctor of assaulting her. Jarre's score helps to underline the cultural differences, by hinting at what is not spoken.

Considered as one of the greatest ever film adaptations, *A Passage to India* was a critical success. *Time* magazine devoted a cover story to Lean's new movie with the headline 'An Old Master's New Triumph', and the film was nominated for eleven Academy Awards, including

Best Picture. Lean, who received his knighthood in the year of the film's release, was nominated for three of them, Best Director, Best Editing and Best Adapted Screenplay, although *A Passage to India* was victorious only for Peggy Ashcroft for Best Supporting Actress and, yet again for Jarre, Best Original Score. Clearly, the collaboration between the composer and director produced magical alchemy, and Jarre credited Lean with setting the bar so high that he delivered a score that matched the quality of the film: 'David Lean once said to me, "Maurice, you are the doctor of the film." It is true that music can help a scene run more smoothly, but it has to be a good film for the music to have its best effect. Music can cure a minor sickness but it cannot help the terminally ill!'

❧

One of the earliest partnerships in this book, the rapport between David Lean and Maurice Jarre may feel more formal in comparison to others here. The two weren't 'buddies' in the sense of popping round on a Sunday night to listen to tunes in the composer's garage, and Jarre was not involved as a sounding board for the early development of the films. There were no on-set visits, no on-screen cameos for the composer, no interviews describing each other as a brother: this was a relationship based on a clear respect for the scale of the other's talents, though that is not to say that they did not have a bond beyond the purely professional. Described by Jarre as 'a master of cinema, a model of rigour and professionalism in the service of cinema', Lean had a reputation for demanding the best, and woe betide you if you were a crew or cast member who could not deliver. The fact he kept returning to Jarre says it all. Their success suggests that perhaps a close personal chemistry between composer and director isn't essential; what might be more important is to have clear, shared goals for the task at hand and for both parties to work hard to achieve them. Nevertheless, there was a fondness there, and the composer was on course to score Lean's next project, an adaptation of *Nostromo* by Joseph Conrad, before the director's death from pneumonia in 1991 ended the superb collaboration.

Although Jarre also worked with other legendary directors such as Alfred Hitchcock (*Topaz*) and collaborated on three films with John Huston and five with Peter Weir, including the acclaimed scores for *Witness* and *Dead Poets Society*, he often cited Lean as one of the directors he admired the most.

After Lean's death, Jarre said, 'I owe him everything . . . He gave me the best pictures, the opportunity to receive three Oscars for four films – not so bad! – and he gave me his friendship. He was a gentleman. When I lost him, I lost not only a great director, but a great friend.' In 1992, the composer conducted the Royal Philharmonic Orchestra in a special tribute concert at the Barbican in London, featuring his scores for the four films. He was visibly moved at the end, addressing the audience, 'Thank you. I think David would be happy.'

 ## Collaboration History

*Lawrence of Arabia* (1962)
*Doctor Zhivago* (1965)
*Ryan's Daughter* (1970)
*A Passage to India* (1984)

 ## Suggested Playlist

*Lawrence of Arabia*, Overture
*Lawrence of Arabia*, Main Theme

*Lawrence of Arabia*, That is the Desert

*Lawrence of Arabia*, First Entrance to the Desert – Night and Star –
   Lawrence and Tafas

*Doctor Zhivago*, Overture

*Doctor Zhivago*, Main Title

*Doctor Zhivago*, Kontakion – Funeral Song

*Doctor Zhivago*, Lara's Theme

*Doctor Zhivago*, Then It's A Gift (End Title)

*Ryan's Daughter*, Rosy's Theme

*A Passage to India*, A Passage to India

*A Passage to India*, Adela's Theme

*A Passage to India*, Bicycle Ride

# 8

# THOMAS NEWMAN
# AND SAM MENDES

*'Looking and listening
every step of the way'*

Ayoung British theatre director making his debut feature-length film and an established composer from a Hollywood musical dynasty: the writing was not necessarily on the wall for Sam Mendes and Thomas Newman to forge a long-lasting partnership, but after the runaway success of their first collaboration, *American Beauty* (1999), Newman has provided the music for all of Mendes' films that have required a score – that's six out of the seven: the Depression-era crime tale *Road to Perdition* (2002), biographical war drama *Jarhead* (2005), a tale of the suburban American Dream gone wrong, *Revolutionary Road* (2008), and two James Bond blockbusters *Skyfall* (2012) and *Spectre* (2015). As Mendes has described their collaboration, 'It has ended up being, not through any design, just accidentally and totally for the right reasons, one of the longest and most rewarding artistic relationships of my life. Every movie has been a journey, and every movie we've found new things, and the

135

day that I would want to stop working with Tom is the day that we both look at each other and say, "Well, there's nothing in here that we haven't done before." So what's their secret?

With different backgrounds and a decade between them, the root of the Newman–Mendes partnership appears to lie in a mutual appreciation rather than similar upbringing or implicit shared experiences. They are two thoroughly charming gents, both genuinely generous in their praise of the other, and their collaboration is undoubtedly strengthened by the fact they have not fallen into a symbiotic working relationship but have plenty of their own projects on the go. Sam's stage work spans William Shakespeare to Roald Dahl, with successful productions of *Richard III*, *King Lear* and *Charlie and the Chocolate Factory* in recent years, and in 2017 he directed the Royal Court Theatre's fastest-selling play to date, *The Ferryman* by Jez Butterworth. Thomas has an impressively varied CV that features animation (*Wall-E*, *Finding Nemo*), drama (*The Help*, *Erin Brockovich*), comedy (the *Best Exotic Marigold Hotel* series), biopics (*The Iron Lady*), and documentaries (*He Named Me Malala*). There is clearly no shortage of composing work for him and he's earned enough Academy Award nominations to no doubt feel intense pressure to win one: his most recent Best Original Score nod, for *Passengers* in 2017, was his thirteenth in the category.

⁓

Before turning to the first collaboration, let's get up to speed with the Newman family to understand why the surname holds such clout in Hollywood. Alfred Newman, Thomas's father, was Head of Music at 20th Century Fox from 1940 to 1960 and the recipient of nine Academy Awards – more than any other music director or composer. His brothers Lionel and Emil, Thomas's uncles, were also composers and conductors, and Lionel was nominated for eleven Oscars, winning for *Hello Dolly!* with Lennie Hayton in 1969. Thomas's cousin, the singer-songwriter Randy Newman, has picked up two Oscars from an impressive twenty nominations, and has added his musical touch to seven Disney Pixar films including the *Toy Story* trilogy. Joey Newman, first cousin once removed, is also a composer, as is Thomas's brother David, who has scored around a hundred films, and Thomas's sister Maria is a critically acclaimed violinist, violist and pianist.

Perhaps it was inevitable that Newman would become a film composer, but what a weight of expectation! Speaking in 2014, he acknowledged the pressure: 'It was a career I never thought I wanted to go into for probably just that reason. It was a long-cast shadow, but somehow I ended up in it!' He was fourteen when Alfred died and although he'd seen some of his father's films, it was only in his mid-teens that he 'started to drift into a sense of what it meant to be a creative person, which had never occurred to me growing up. What is it to be creative, what is it to have an idea, no one had ever really talked about that.'

Despite the pressures of living up to the family name, Newman had the freedom to develop his own style, one that is now instantly discernible and often imitated: 'I always had a voice, but I don't think I really knew it, and as a student I was quite shy and probably felt at the bottom of the class, and maybe that turned me into a good listener. I think I started to develop a sense of aesthetics and I started to learn what I liked, and I just went for it.' The skill of listening is significant because a typical Thomas Newman score is atmospheric rather than bombastic, with a subtle and an often modern-sounding approach that doesn't veer into nostalgia or familiar 'retro' territory, even if he's scoring a period piece. His preference for percussion and experimenting with eclectic instruments allows for a deftness of touch that never stifles.

Newman has described the spareness of his approach: 'Any time I write, you see an image and you have an idea. Maybe you work on a marimba idea or a piano idea and you put it up against an image and the image tells you something. Maybe it tells you the writing is too dense or too thick and you thin it out or you subtract. So typically I try to have ideas, put them in front of an image, then ask myself why they work or why they don't work. It's less about who I am as a writer, and more who I'm accepting in, what my ears are buying. Early on, I thought no one's listening anyway so why go out of my way to try to impress people, so I tried to subtract, and I guess my sense of harmony became very spare as a result.'

It goes without saying that he had an easier entry into the film industry than most. One of his first jobs was a cue on *Return of the Jedi*, thanks to Uncle Lionel who was musical supervisor on the first three *Star Wars* films and a close friend of John Williams. Not many aspiring composers get their work experience by orchestrating the death of Lord Vader, but Newman went on to build his own reputation and by the time he met Sam Mendes, he'd been composing for film for well over a decade, with *The Player* (1992), *The Horse Whisperer* (1998) and *Meet Joe Black* (1998) under his belt, along with Oscar nominations for *The Shawshank Redemption* (1994), *Little Women* (1994) and *Unstrung Heroes* (1995).

⟨⟩

Thomas Newman's and Sam Mendes' first collaboration was one of the defining films of the 1990s, with music to match. Picking up five Academy Awards, including Best Director, Best Picture and Best Original Screenplay, *American Beauty* (1999) was a landmark moment in the careers of both composer and director. Speaking to Andrew Collins before the release of *Spectre*, Mendes said, 'You've got to remember, I was

Thomas Newman and Sam Mendes at the premiere
afterparty of *Revolutionary Road*, 2008.

a first-time film-maker and was asking somebody who'd just composed
music for *The Shawshank Redemption* and all these wonderful scores to
do my small movie, so he gave me my break in a way!'

Newman shared his memories of meeting Mendes: 'I was in the middle of *The Green Mile* and there was a bit of a hiatus when they decided
if they wanted Tom Hanks to dress up as an old person to play himself,
or if they were going to cast another part, so there was a seven- or eight-
week break and I wanted to do something quick and different. My agent
suggested *American Beauty*, which was just beginning to happen, and I
went and met with Sam in an office building in Wilshire Boulevard in
Los Angeles, and we hit it off.' The original brief was for Newman to
provide music to fill in the gaps between country-and-western songs that
were due to feature because lead character Lester Burnham was described

in the script as a fan of the genre. However, as the composer recalls, the musical direction changed after Mendes returned to England: 'It was him, I think, who wanted to have the things percuss and bang and bonk and move forward with a kind of pace.'

While Mendes had attracted admirers for his successful stage productions of the musicals *Oliver!* and *Cabaret*, the film studio had offered the role to about twenty other directors including Mike Nichols and Robert Zemeckis. Mendes' agent, Beth Swofford, was arranging meetings with studio figures to discuss potential directorial roles for him, and the story goes that he picked out *American Beauty* from a pile of scripts and knew that this was the one for him. DreamWorks Pictures had bought the story by Alan Ball, so Mendes met up with DreamWorks co-founder Steven Spielberg and, after receiving his encouragement, successfully pitched for the role of director.

Some might have wondered whether an Englishman was the right person for the job of bringing the story of a midlife crisis in the American suburbs to life, but the distance perhaps played to Mendes' strengths. As Newman notes, 'Sam's very observant, I think, culturally and emotionally – that's one of his talents.' These powers of observation, combined with the composer's awareness of the importance of listening, made for a fertile collaborative environment. The composer was impressed from the start by the director's intuitive approach to the scoring process: 'He was a very quick learner in terms of knowing how malleable music could be and how malleable post-production could be; how you could make something slightly different than the intention ... He has an amazing work ethic, an amazing way of knowing how to bring good things out of people.'

In Mendes' words, 'You really are in the hands of another creative force when you're working with a composer ... I think when you get that feeling that the music has a life of its own when added to the visuals, that's the work of someone with a real gift. It isn't always the work of someone who's shadowing the movie with music all the time . . . So it was a process of discovery for me, to try and work out where and how I felt I wanted music to be used.'

The *American Beauty* score contains some of the most recognised – and imitated – film cues around today, seeping into popular culture and even spawning a dance song, 'American Dream' by Jakatta. Initially Newman's music gives the impression of a light veneer, but the use and layering of unusual instruments provide a resonance and texture that pulse throughout the film. It is never overpowering, yet asserts prominence within key scenes. 'American Beauty' is often referred to as 'the plastic bag theme' because we hear it when teenagers Ricky and Jane are watching a video made by Ricky of a plastic bag seemingly dancing in the wind. The composer is modest when asked about what is now considered to be a quintessentially Newman cue: 'It's not like you ever look at these things and say, "Aha! Here's my moment!"' According to Mendes, 'I remember the piece that accompanies Lester's fantasy of Angela on the ceiling in the rose petals being an absolutely perfect piece of music. It's probably only forty-five seconds long but it's just exquisite . . . That's what you hope for, and a lot of the time with Tom, that's what you get.'

Newman struggled, however, with the film's opening cue 'Dead Already'. After fifteen or sixteen attempts that all received a lukewarm response from the director, he knew he was running out of time, and luckily the percussionist Michael Fisher stepped in: 'He was the one who said, "Let's play with tablas", and that's very much the case with my players. I really try to invite ideas from them, and it just kind of came together. I finally had the guts to play it to Sam and he liked it!' Mendes recalls, 'I put in all the other pieces of music and mixed the whole movie while he was still trying to write that piece. In fact, the last piece of music that went onto the picture at the very end of the mix was that opening piece. He nailed it right at the end, and when he finally wrote it he said something like "This is it. If you don't like it, I give up" – and luckily I liked it!'

⋙

The duo's next collaboration was the Depression-era gangster film ***Road to Perdition*** (2002), starring Tom Hanks, Jude Law and future James Bond Daniel Craig. Newman returned to the more orchestral style of *The Shawshank Redemption* for this story set in the organised crime world of 1930s Chicago. It's an assured score, with the composer's stylistic mannerisms well placed within the broader orchestral realm. Dark and gloomy elements suit the revenge theme of the film, yet it's not without moments of humour and surprise. The Irishness of the Chicago setting is hinted at with the appearance of pennywhistle and pipe in 'Rock Island, 1931', but these are carefully placed rather than overbearing. Another highlight, 'Road to Chicago', begins with a piano before introducing multi-layered strings and the title cue, which provides hope tinged with melancholy.

Mendes explained that he doesn't follow a set pattern in his films, and doesn't expect the composer to either: 'I don't use what I would consider the same box of tricks for each movie. For example, *American Beauty* was very still, very composed; *Road to Perdition* had a much broader scope, much bigger landscapes, much fuller, much more symphonic. *Jarhead* was all hand-held cameras, there are no right-angles in the movie anywhere, so there's something a bit more rough and improvised, whereas there was nothing improvised about *Road to Perdition* at all. You could use those analogies exactly the same way with music: you're using chamber music for *American Beauty*, there's glassy strings, things that hover and shiver but nothing overtly emotional, and very few big statements. There's mischief in the music, there's quirkiness, there's oddness and I think originality, whereas with *Road to Perdition* it's much grander. Often Tom's trademark bowed and strummed instruments, but always sitting within a broader, more sweeping gesture. And then with *Jarhead*, you've got something much more eclectic: you've got guitars and odd use of Middle Eastern instruments, and strange bowed, strangely surreal sounds. A fragmented score for a fragmented movie and a fragmented narrative.'

Based on the best-selling 2003 memoir by Anthony Swofford, who served in the first Gulf War, *Jarhead* (2005) is a study of the psychological effects of warfare. Focusing on the personal experience of one soldier, played by Jake Gyllenhaal, it captures the heat, boredom, loneliness and exhaustion experienced by the soldiers, and the music serves to mirror these frustrations. Working with his regular musicians, Newman created a multicultural soundboard, merging boundaries to reflect the soldiers' backgrounds and current location. The director is full of praise for Newman's skilled multi-instrumentalists and describes sitting in on some of the recording sessions as 'a real thrill': 'If you say something like "It needs to feel a little bit more mischievous there, when that happens", then someone will have an idea and the piece will be adapted and suddenly it will come to life or it will catch the light in a different way.' A quick scan of the *Jarhead* credits reveals a number of unusual instruments and effects, with George Doering playing the esraj, reverse hammer dulcimer and bowed cumbus, among others; Rick Cox tackling the processed xaphoons and ambient elements, and the aforementioned Michael Fisher looking after daf, riq, wave drum and crotales. Not your typical film score. It's a curious listen and by no means an easy one, with electronic cues like 'Full Chemical Gear' providing a more masculine sound, 'Listen Up' nodding to Eminem's 'Lose Yourself' with its swagger, and pieces like 'Dead Anyway' offering eerie soundscapes.

By his own admission, the composer enjoys the challenge of exploring and creating different sound worlds through experimental scores such as *Jarhead*: 'The idea of colour excites me, the idea of seeing where I end up as opposed to assuming where I'll go. This idea of un-intention, of being unintended in my approach and then listening to something that I write and putting it against an image and asking myself if it works and why. Instead of saying, "OK, I'm going to sit down with manuscript in hand and I'm going to write my piece", which is typically what we think of as a composer's role . . . for me, it's always finding an idea and grabbing it and stuffing it in my ears.'

❧

Mendes and Newman returned to themes of suburban dissatisfaction with **Revolutionary Road** (2008), considered by many as a companion piece to *American Beauty*. Adapted from the acclaimed debut novel by Richard Yates, this is the story of Frank and April Wheeler, played by Leonardo DiCaprio and Kate Winslet, who live in Connecticut in the 1950s and plan to move to Paris to escape, as Frank puts it, 'the hopeless emptiness' of their life – and the composer provided a suitably unsettling and claustrophobic score, steeped in sadness. The haunting 'Revolutionary Road (End Title)' ranks among his finest; 'The Bright Young Man' offers brightness in the piano tune but seems purposefully lacking in warmth, with the percussion keeping the audience at arm's length, and another stand-out cue, 'Golden People', captures the feeling of being an observer of this apparently perfect marriage, somehow conjuring elements of envy between the pauses.

Mendes had a particular idea in mind for the music: 'I was very conscious when we did *Revolutionary Road* that we work off a single theme, primarily, in a way that was quite old-fashioned. You have your tune for the movie, you develop that tune, you repeat it, sometimes you play it on a single piano, sometimes with a full orchestra, and all the ranges in between. And you hope that that tune expresses both the beauty and the sadness of the story, and both the love affair and the tragedy simultaneously, depending on how it's delivered and orchestrated. So we took that one theme and we manipulated it and changed it and Tom varied it with great skill throughout the movie so it had a kind of changing aspect along with the changing fortunes of Frank and April.'

By this stage, with four collaborations between them, Newman could have felt relatively confident in his role as Mendes' go-to composer, but he has never allowed himself to get too comfortable or to assume that the relationship will continue from strength to strength: 'You still have to perform. There's going to be a moment when you're in a room with him and he's not going to like something you're doing. You presume nothing about that relationship other than that you're grateful for it, but I still have to honour the composer–director relationship and try as hard as I can, and guide him if I feel he needs guidance but also bow to his visions if that's the thing to do.'

Arguably their two most recent films, involving British super spy and cultural institution James Bond, were steeped in more pressure than the others put together. As soon as Sam Mendes was announced as the director of the twenty-third official Bond film, *Skyfall* (2012), fans wondered if his usual musical collaborator would join him. Could a composer who was so well known for his minimal, atmospheric style take on 007 and all the stylistic expectations that go with the franchise? 'The big question for me was, was he going to be able to carry over into the Bond world?' admitted the director. 'Because it's a big ask. He had to adapt and use the great John Barry stuff and the Monty Norman theme, and that's a tricky balance for a composer. One of the great thrills for me, because I stood by him and insisted that we used him, is how amazingly he pulled it off.'

Mendes continues, 'There's a certain amount about his work that is consistent across all the films but then there's a certain amount that doesn't sound like Tom Newman at all. Maybe retrospectively you hear the score for *American Beauty* and go, "That's Tom Newman", but at the time it was quite original. But I've always loved pushing Tom in new directions in the way that I was pushing myself. The most recent example of that is working with him on Bond. He'd never done a big action adventure movie before, and neither had I!'

Newman recalls his initial conversation with Mendes about Bond: 'I called him up and said, "Listen, I don't know if you would ever consider me for this but I would love to be a part of it if you would have me", and he had had it in his mind that he wanted to work with me and Roger Deakins [the cinematographer who had worked on *Jarhead* and *Revolutionary Road*], and bring us along. Which was flattering on the one hand, but on the other, did I understand the Englishness enough of the Bond experience, and could I do it? . . . I knew I was going to live or die in the arena of "Does it work or does it not?"'

By focusing on the task at hand, the composer was able to approach the scoring for *Skyfall* as he would for any other movie: 'You get signed to do the film, you read the script, maybe you start seeing little bits of picture. It wasn't long after they wrapped that I came to London where I was for two or three weeks before Sam had an opportunity to even see me because he was so busy editing. And then you just go to work. Sam's so specific, he's so meticulous with his sense of music and how it aligns with action, that he's just looking and listening every step of the way. As the cut refines, so does the music, and then you're into a period of time where he's really weighing in, in terms of what you're doing.'

As Mendes recalls, 'Tom, who's supremely gifted, sometimes needed to be convinced, cajoled, into using bigger guns, bigger artillery in terms of the sheer muscle required to rise above the sound landscape of an action movie. You needed big traceable percussion beats that run under things, that bind sequences together, you need to not be afraid of using horns and some of the more muscular sounds that are available to you in a big orchestra. But then there's delicacy too and still the confidence – I mean, one of the pieces I love most in *Skyfall* is the confidence to empty out and go to a single tone, something that really is haunting and strange: when Bond goes to Skyfall, to Scotland, for the first time, the score there is mesmerisingly simple and hypnotic. It's a sort of counter-intuitive choice you get from somebody with Tom's taste and keen eye for the unexpected. You don't get, "Oh great, it's a big shot of a car driving across a landscape, let's hammer in with eighty strings"; instead you get this shivering, strange tone that makes it feel that he's going back in time. It did everything that a bigger piece would do, but more, and it was not a cliché. That's the other thing: he has a remarkably keen eye for moving away from the clichéd and the obvious, in terms of musical language.'

As Mendes points out, the composer successfully created a Bond score and a Thomas Newman score, with the occasional nod to his predecessors David Arnold and John Barry, as well as the required incorporation of Monty Norman's original Bond theme, while cues such as 'She's Mine' shine with brassy flourishes. Newman was careful in his preparation, admitting, 'Immersion scares me because then you start to really feel the weight of what's gone before. I did a lot of listening, but

I didn't do such serious listening that I felt burdened by it.' Just before the film's release, he said that the whole experience had been 'amazing' but tough: 'It's a lot of work that comes down the pipe very late, so you're really up against a huge mountain of work over a small period of time, and that's daunting.' The *Skyfall* title tune is put to superb use in 'Komodo Dragon'; 'Quartermaster' goes at a real pace with layered, jangly sounds; and another highlight, 'Tennyson', feels like a trademark Bond action cue, appearing in a key scene in which Judi Dench's character M defends the role of the secret service as Javier Bardem's villain gets ever closer. While other composers might have thrown down the gauntlet and brought in bombastic crescendos, Newman never overdoes it, allowing the on-screen action to speak for itself.

*Skyfall* was the first James Bond film to take over $1 billion worldwide and was the highest-grossing film in the UK until *Star Wars: The Force Awakens* knocked it into second place three years later. It also won critical acclaim and picked up two Academy Awards and two BAFTAs, including Best Original Score for Thomas Newman. When it was announced that Mendes would return to the franchise to direct the follow-up, it was taken as given that the composer would join him.

The director is particularly proud of the score for **Spectre** (2015), describing it as 'much more effortlessly muscular and wide-screen and cool' than some of *Skyfall*. He points to the balance Newman achieves between different instruments and themes, particularly in the opening ten minutes where he weaves the Bond theme in and out of drum music on the streets in Mexico. 'If you study it as a soundscape – holding off the music during the foot chase through the streets and the beginning of the fight in the helicopter, then when it comes back in with this immense force during the second half of the helicopter fight – the courage to drop music out during action and then bring it back in again, that came with both of us in the second movie. The danger with action music is you're trying to pump false energy into stuff that feels like it hasn't quite earned it, and so you're having to push the music to fill in the gaps that the physical action is not succeeding on illustrating, whereas in *Spectre* . . . I felt like it was there at the right time.'

Other highlights include 'The Pale King', which makes a bold entrance before ultimately tiptoeing into the musical shadows, the gentle 'Madeleine' and more experimentation with signature brass elements and the Monty Norman theme in 'Westminster Bridge'. Perhaps second time around, Newman was more used to blending in *that* music into his own score: 'The idea of Bond is so much bigger than I am that you kind of have to allow it at all times and swallow it up and enjoy it.'

When asked what directors should look for in a composer to achieve a fruitful working partnership, Mendes offers this advice: 'Ultimately, it's an entirely personal thing. One person's Mozart is another person's Salieri! Some people hear truth; some people hear fakery. Don't look at their list of credits, don't look at what they've done in the past, just close your eyes and listen. Do you like it? Does it speak to you? Does it feel like your movie? Then, meet them. Do you talk the same language? If you don't, don't be ashamed to say, "Thanks very much, but I don't talk Newman, and you don't talk Mendes", but if you feel you have a shared way of communicating about music, and you get on – because you spend a lot of time biffing things back and forth in a room – that's a good sign.' He also rates honesty in both directions, describing the ideal composer as 'not someone you can push around, not somebody who is scared of telling you that they want you to give this piece of music another shot'.

Mendes continues: 'But the most important of all is you've got to have a sense of humour! You've got to be able to laugh because making a movie is not easy. You have to be able to get perspective on it at some point because otherwise you can all get things out of proportion. Tom is extremely funny and witty, in an extremely dry and self-deprecating way, but he does make me laugh a lot and I hope I [make him laugh a lot] too, although possibly less than [he does me]!'

It's evident that both director and composer get stuck in, never simply going through the motions. Newman reckons their collaboration works so well because 'we have a sense of style, I can put feeling into his images' but it's significant that he acknowledges the role of a composer within the bigger picture: 'It's not about you, it's about the film or the image and how much can you adapt to it.' Their other projects, from Mendes' stage productions to Newman's regular scoring work for directors like Steven Soderbergh and John Madden, have allowed for some space over the decades, which may have helped keep things harmonious. According to the director, 'We've had some adventures together, and we know each other now very well. It's quite eccentric now, our working relationship, and it would be quite unlike anyone else's. If I worked with another composer, I'm sure it would be very different, and when he works with other directors, I'm sure that relationship is very different. But we get a kick out of working with each other. We're yet to get bored of each other, so I hope that continues!'

 ## Collaboration History

*American Beauty* (1999)
*Road to Perdition* (2002)
*Jarhead* (2005)

*Revolutionary Road* (2008)
*Skyfall* (2012)
*Spectre* (2015)

 ## Suggested Playlist

*American Beauty*, Dead Already
*American Beauty*, Any Other Name
*American Beauty*, American Beauty
*Road to Perdition*, Rock Island, 1931
*Road to Perdition*, Road to Perdition
*Jarhead*, Unsick Most Ricky-Tick
*Jarhead*, Dead Anyway
*Revolutionary Road*, The Bright Young Man
*Revolutionary Road*, Golden People
*Revolutionary Road*, Revolutionary Road (End Title)
*Skyfall*, Komodo Dragon
*Skyfall*, Quartermaster
*Skyfall*, Tennyson
*Skyfall*, She's Mine
*Spectre*, Westminster Bridge
*Spectre*, The Pale King
*Spectre*, Madeleine

# 9

# HOWARD SHORE
# AND PETER JACKSON

*'A meeting of minds'*

*I*f you ever need convincing of the power of film music, listen to the opening bars of 'The Breaking of the Fellowship' from *The Fellowship of the Ring* (2001), the first in *The Lord of the Rings* trilogy, and you'll be transported to Middle-earth faster than you can say J. R. R. Tolkien. The music and films brought that fantasy world to life so perfectly that composer Howard Shore and director Peter Jackson cemented their place in cinematic history with their combined eye and ear for detail, and they returned to the Shire the following decade with *The Hobbit* trilogy. Previously both had achieved some success with individual projects, such as Jackson's horror-comedy *Braindead* and psychological drama *Heavenly Creatures,* and Shore's extensive work with fellow Canadian director David Cronenberg on unsettling films including *The Fly* and *Crash*, but together they proved themselves masters of Tolkien's realm.

The composer's and director's greatest joint achievement lies in the very scale of the project. The original book, *The Fellowship of the Ring*, which introduced the world to this classic tale of good and evil, loyalty and friendship, and survival and courage, was published in 1954 and took Tolkien fourteen years to write. Peter Jackson and his co-writers and producers Fran Walsh and Philippa Boyens spent three years working on the screenplays for the trilogy, and the filming in Jackson's native New Zealand was a hugely ambitious project, building a fantasy landscape. They filmed the three movies back to back and, at around fourteen months, it is the longest shoot in history. Jackson described it as a major endeavour during the post-production of *The Fellowship of the Ring*, 'just in terms of the physical endurance, mental endurance, the stress and sheer size and scope of it. From that point of view it has been like a siege, a marathon – it has been gruelling.'

And then there's the score, which comes to an immense ten hours for the complete box sets. Add in Shore's work for *The Hobbit* trilogy and we're in the region of twenty-one hours of music, with well over a hundred leitmotifs for characters, cultures, objects and events. Considering the large scale required for every aspect of the production (costumes and prop-wise, we're talking 48,000 pieces of armour, around 19,000 costumes and 1,800 pairs of hobbit feet for the lead actors, and that's just for starters), it is hardly surprising that this was not simply a collaboration between director and composer, but rather an involved group dynamic with, according to Jackson, 'a wonderful family-like feeling': 'There was no room for anyone to be a prima donna or to be difficult, because we were all together for so long.'

*The Lord of the Rings* series, aided by the *Harry Potter* films, reignited a love for the fantasy genre and brought about a renewed interest in Tolkien's books. Unadjusted for inflation, it is the highest-grossing film trilogy worldwide of all time, ahead of the original *Star Wars* and *The Godfather* trilogies. It is the fifth-highest-grossing film franchise of all time – a feat that's all the more impressive considering that the *James Bond* series, which is in fourth place, encompasses twenty-six movies but this covers only seven (Jackson's six films are grouped together with the 1978 animation). As well as striking box-office gold, the critical praise and awards rolled in and *The Lord of the Rings* won seventeen out of thirty Academy Award nominations – a record for any trilogy – with *The Hobbit* films later bringing the total number of nominations to thirty-seven. The third and final *Lord of the Rings* film, *The Return of the King*, won an unprecedented eleven Oscars from eleven nominations, including Best Original Score for Howard Shore, who had received the same award for *The Fellowship of the Ring*. All three films won the Grammy Award for Best Score Soundtrack Album, and Shore's music for the trilogy has been the highest-placed film score in the Classic FM Hall of Fame, the annual poll to discover listeners' musical tastes, every year since 2003. The music is ageless, somehow inseparable from the films yet resoundingly powerful in its own right.

⌇

The young Peter Jackson was fascinated with Ray Harryhausen films and comedies such as *Monty Python's Flying Circus* but it was the original *King Kong* that inspired him to pursue a career as a movie director. He loved photography, and when he was eight, a family friend gave him a Super 8 camera. A fan of 'Hammer Horrors', one of Jackson's first home-made films, *Curse of the Gravewalker*, was about vampires, though he never completed it. (Decades later, when he cast Christopher Lee in *The Lord of the Rings*, he was tempted to see if the actor could provide a cameo as Dracula so that he could finally finish the job.)

When Jackson left school and was working at the local Wellington newspaper, he saved up to buy filming equipment and was particularly interested in special-effects processes and techniques. His first film, 'splatstick' horror-comedy *Bad Taste* (1987), might not seem an obvious debut for one of the most bankable directors in the world, but Jackson's career continued with projects that mixed comedy and horror to differing degrees, such as the aforementioned *Braindead*, known as *Dead Alive* in North America, and *Meet the Feebles* (1989). The director built a reputation for himself with *Heavenly Creatures* (1994), for which he and his partner Fran Walsh received an Oscar nomination for Best Original Screenplay, and after that success he was able to make his first big-budget Hollywood film, *The Frighteners* (1996), on which Robert Zemeckis served as executive producer. He collaborated with New Zealand-born composer Peter Dasent on three of his early films, but after acquiring the film rights to Tolkien's book and embarking on a project far greater than anything he'd worked on before, he was looking for an experienced composer.

Howard Shore has experience by the bucketful. He began his career as a performer, as so many film composers do, playing saxophone in a band called The Lighthouse. They opened for Jimi Hendrix, toured with Jefferson Airplane, and in a concert in Philadelphia were even supported by Elton John! Shore moved into the world of television when his school friend Lorne Michaels invited him to work on *Saturday Night Live*. As music director for the hit US show, the composer soon learned about musical improvisation and, no doubt, how to work under pressure, and he scored his first film, *I Miss You, Hugs and Kisses*, in 1978. He had composed about sixty or seventy scores before Tolkien came calling, so while it may be easy to think of him now solely as the 'Middle-earth' composer, it's worth remembering his output spans horror (*Se7en*), comedy (*Mrs Doubtfire*), real-life dramas (*Spotlight*) and even 'tween' romances

(*The Twilight Saga: Eclipse*). Whether his music is unsettling or light, there is a real poise to Shore's scores and he brings a conscientious approach to each of his projects.

Shore had already scored film adaptations of popular texts, from *The Silence of the Lambs* to *Looking for Richard*, based on Shakespeare's *Richard III*, and he willingly immerses himself in the original source material. Speaking in 2015 about his early work with David Cronenberg, he described himself as an avid reader drawn to projects that required research: 'I really like to delve into the subtext, the dreamlike world that cinema creates, and I'm very happy in that world. So whatever David was interested in, I became interested in, and we did a lot of literary adaptations together like *Crash* and *Naked Lunch*.'

❧

Howard Shore's music appeared in ***The Fellowship of the Ring*** (2001) before he even knew about the film because Peter Jackson and his team used his cues from *Crash*, *The Silence of the Lambs*, *Before and After*, *The Client* and *The Fly* in their temp score after the first couple of months of shooting. Despite being very different projects thematically, the director explained why these scores had such an appeal: 'Howard's music from other films had a mystery, a dark beauty to it, which is his style. It's emotional and his music very much connects with the heart. I really liked what some of his older pieces were actually doing to our picture. It became a natural idea at that stage to have a conversation with Howard.' He was also aware he needed someone who could engage fully with the demands of the project, 'who would be prepared to enter into the spirit of the film, to be very committed, to spend more time on the score, to work closely with us, and to be a collaborative member of the team'.

When asked to describe his reaction to the offer of scoring *The Lord of the Rings*, the composer replied, with characteristic calm, 'I had read the book, like so many people, in the 1960s. I didn't know about the film until Peter Jackson called and asked me. He just called to chat, I hadn't really met him until I went to New Zealand, and I met Peter and Fran Walsh and Philippa Boyens, and it was amazing what they were creating. You wanted to be a part of it.' Witnessing the scope of the project, Shore must have seen this as a culmination of everything he'd learned about scoring up to that point, and his preparation involved researching the director's early work, seeking out some of his lesser-known films such as *Forgotten Silver*, as well as undertaking a painstaking study of the text. He apparently spent four months on research before writing a note.

It's inaccurate to refer to **The Two Towers** (2002) and **The Return of the King** (2003) as 'sequels' to *The Fellowship of the Ring*, not only because they were filmed concurrently but because they are essentially three acts to one story, and Shore composed the music with that in mind, knowing the three films would be available to watch in one sitting on DVD.

After the composer's initial visit to the set in 2000, he returned to New Zealand around ten or twelve times during the shoot, immersing himself in the natural landscape and the constructed fantasy worlds. The temp tracks, comprised of his earlier film scores, were a useful starting point for Jackson's and Shore's early discussions, especially for a director who admits 'music is a very difficult thing to communicate about': 'Howard was extremely gracious when it came to the temp. He listened and we discussed why we chose different tracks [and] why a particular piece of temp seems to work.' They would get into a rhythm of long-distance communication when Shore was working back in New York, and the thousands of miles between them might have proved fruitful in that they allowed the composer to retain some objectivity, or overall clarity, about the story, while working firmly within Tolkien's world. Set apart from the daily pressures of the film shoot, Shore could create his large-scale score, bit by bit: 'The task was daunting of course. I mean, the book was one of the classics of the twentieth century, and you had a lot of responsibility to tell the story well, with this much heart and soul and truth that you could put in the music. So I just set about the task, I just immersed myself in Tolkien's world for almost four years.'

Beyond the original text, and the ongoing filming, there were other elements at play that helped Shore: he cites Tolkien illustrators John Howe and Alan Lee, who created a lot of the artwork, as particular inspiration, as well as Richard Taylor, creator of Weta Workshop, who created the actual artefacts of the story: 'The armour, the costumes, a lot of the design work was in his shop, and you could tour and be inspired. So not only were you taking Tolkien's work from the page but you were also seeing how it was going to be brought to the screen.'

The score was to be orchestral, without any electronic accompaniment, because, as Jackson explained, 'The Lord of the Rings reflects a very ancient world so I wanted music that was appropriate to the era. I didn't want anything too revolutionary. I wanted it to feel like it belongs to Middle-earth.' Shore has said it was impossible to approach it as a movie score, likening it more to an opera, with Wagnerian leitmotifs woven within the films for clarity, offering a musical map to help the audience navigate their way through the different cultures and connections. The composer was aware that this was a film for both Tolkien fans and newcomers alike, and aimed to write a score that would honour the book while also bringing it to as broad an audience as possible. As he acknowledges, this was a far more complex story than many of his previous films: 'Film music is very much point of view, and here the point of view was to express the story with as much clarity as possible, to tell Tolkien's great story in a way that audiences would simply understand it if they had not read the book, or if they had read it but didn't remember it.' The intricacies of the leitmotifs, representing entities from the Shire to a sword, and even different aspects of the ring, from the power it wields over certain characters to the evil lying within it, brought out the best in Shore, who seems to have delighted in building this musical universe, with creatively calculated and painstakingly constructed pieces. The musicologist Doug Adams described roughly eighty-seven leitmotifs in his detailed book *The Music of The Lord of the Rings* (2010), although more have been identified, with even more after the release of *The Hobbit* trilogy.

Working between New York and New Zealand, weaving this intricate musical tapestry, discussions became more frequent regarding the placement of music on the screen: 'Peter was really the focus for the spotting, as to where music would actually be in a scene and how it was representing the story. *The Lord of the Rings* is considered one of the most complex fantasy worlds ever created, so it was important to show clarity in the storytelling. We began by using the technique of themes and motifs very early on – we started in the Mines of Moria.' Shore has described how useful he found it to start within the centre of the story and work outwards, and this particular section was recorded with the New Zealand Symphony Orchestra and a sixty-voice Maori Samoan choir in preparation for a screening at the Cannes Film Festival in 2001. At this early stage it was clear that the collaboration involved all three screenwriters, and that the additional input was welcomed by the composer: 'Fran had great perception about the relationships in the story – Gandalf's relationship to Bilbo, Gandalf's relationship to Frodo, Frodo to Bilbo, Sam's relationship to Frodo, all really important to me in developing my musical ideas and in how to structure the piece. Philippa was very well read on the subject of ring mythology, very old concepts of what the ring represented down through the ages, not just in *The Lord of the Rings* but through other mythologies, and she was able to really guide me into the historical nature of the piece.'

Shore's score also leans towards the operatic with the use of voices. Boys' choirs were selected for their purity of sound to depict elements such as the innocence of the hobbits and the friendship between Sam and Frodo. Soloists including Enya and Elizabeth Fraser provided otherworldly, ethereal qualities, and again Philippa Boyens was an influence, steering Shore to experiment with different voices and languages: 'It was through discussions with Philippa that the idea came to use Tolkien's languages, that were so prevalent in the book. His languages were used in poems and song lyrics, and I wanted to put those languages back into the story, and the way I could do that was through the use of the choir, the adult and the children's choir.' Boyens wrote most of the text, a Tolkien scholar was recruited to translate them, and a linguist then taught the choir the correct pronunciation.

The composer started out working with early cuts of the film and later adapted the music to fit, impressing Jackson with his flexible responses to edits or rewrites. By the time he started work, the screenplays had already been written, but because it had initially been planned as a two-part series, then just one film, and finally a trilogy, there were countless changes made during filming. 'The beautiful thing about our process was if edit changes were made,' he recalls, 'I would go back into the studio and re-record. During the compositional process, which is really the creation of the music, when you're spotting with the director, you're asking the questions, "Why is there music? What is it accomplishing in the scene?" You have to ask the general question as to which point of view in the scene is the music most representing.' Here concise communication – being able to explain what was required for each scene, each piece, to convey – was key.

Shore points to a pivotal scene in *The Fellowship of the Ring*, where Frodo stands before the Council of Elrond and says, 'I will take the ring.' 'It's edited with glances and gestures: you glance at Gandalf, a gesture from Aragorn, and you see his friends looking at Frodo in a way that had to be captured in music. This had to be composed in a way that was very specific to the editing. I recall working very hard on this particular scene with Peter, just to make sure that all of those glances, the way the scene unfolded, was done in a perfect way.'

Jackson particularly enjoyed partaking in the musical aspects of production because he had become so used to being the one in control of the film shoot, giving steers and feedback and orders, yet when he sat in on the recording sessions, the composer was in charge, and Jackson was fascinated to watch him in action: 'One of the things I learned from Howard was how much modification can be made when you're actually on the score stage. I had this preconception that all the work is done beforehand and when you get onto the scoring stage there's only a limited amount of further work that can be done. Howard conducts his own scores, so he's totally in command of what happens in every way. To me it was interesting to find out that creativity doesn't necessarily come to an end on the scoring stage.'

Shore consciously creates an environment that is conducive to adaptation, and he believes 'recording is very much a search for the great performance. I like to keep things buoyant and creative, right up to the final dub.' He holds the London Philharmonic Orchestra, with whom he has a long-standing association, in extremely high regard, having first worked with them on *The Fly*. The LPO was the principal orchestra on

Howard Shore and Peter Jackson while working on
*The Lord of the Rings: The Return of the King*, 2003.

the *Lord of the Rings* trilogy and on the first *Hobbit* film, and Shore has
said he wrote the music specifically for the ensemble.

Jackson has claimed the crew found the production of *The Two Towers*
the most difficult of the three films because they felt it had less of an
impactful beginning or end, but Shore's music helps create an effortless
transition to part two, welcoming back the audience and tacitly reminding them of the connections between characters and cultures. Before he
started composing, he asked to watch a rough cut of *The Return of the*

*King*, so he could get the third act of the story in his mind. The director was in London for the recording sessions for the three films because, as he sees it, 'part of the job is supporting the composer', and he adapted the order in which he edited *The Two Towers* to assist Shore. Jackson was mindful that because he had been attending awards ceremonies to receive accolades for *The Fellowship of the Ring*, he had fallen behind on the edit, so when Shore asked for the film's final scenes first, he obliged: 'He said, "I'd like to write the climatic music, and then go back and fill in the pieces in the middle." So at that point I jumped ahead and cut the last couple of reels of the film for Howard. I adjusted the order of my editing because it made sense to Howard.'

Due to tighter deadlines, Shore and Jackson honed their working methods, and the composer's ability to respond quickly to changes proved vital. He would re-score pieces from scenes that had been edited in the morning, write up the amended pieces after the session and record them with the orchestra the next day. The experience was gruelling, with both director and composer working sixteen-hour days over a period of five or six weeks.

A continued extension of the musical universe, the score for *The Two Towers* is a popular choice whenever Classic FM devotes *Saturday Night at the Movies* to the *Lord of the Rings* films, and it is always difficult to fit in the many listener requests, with 'The White Rider', 'The Riders of Rohan' and 'Forth Eorlingas' remaining firm favourites. While it might lack the initial invention of *The Fellowship of the Ring* and the grandeur of *The Return of the King*, it is perhaps the most intriguing of the three scores. Shore was not eligible for the Academy Awards due to a rule forbidding sequel scores that incorporate themes from the previous film, but that was revised the following year so he was allowed to enter for *The Return of the King*, for which he duly won two awards: Best Original Score and, along with Fran Walsh and Annie Lennox, Best Original Song for 'Into the West'.

It definitely feels as though Shore pulled out all the stops for the final instalment in the trilogy, whether to match the required emotions and resolutions within the third act or perhaps because he was by now completely entrenched in the fantasy world: 'By the time we got to the final film,' he reflects, 'we were really working as a great team . . . It took almost four years to compose, orchestrate, and then to conduct the piece and to record and produce the recordings. During that period, we worked out a very fluid method, where I would play Peter new pieces. We would have a note or two on that, I would make some changes on the way themes and motifs were used in the scene, tempos might be adjusted for editing. It was an ongoing process, right into the recording, where Peter would always allow me to do the best performance that I could with the orchestra.'

While Shore started scoring the middle of *The Fellowship of the Ring* and worked his way out, he started at the end and the beginning simultaneously for *The Return of the King*. Jackson was conscious that the music for the end was crucial, describing the final forty minutes as 'the most important music of all three films', so their work on this part was particularly thorough. The score retains a sense of vitality throughout the trilogy, in part due to the introduction of new guest soloists such as Renée Fleming and Sir James Galway in *The Return of the King*. With highlights like 'The Lighting of the Beacons', 'Twilight and Shadow' and 'The Return of the King', it is accomplished and confident, and the quantity of the contributors reflects the scale of the production: 'I was working with very large forces: we always had a palette of 230 musicians. It was a ninety-six-piece symphony orchestra, a sixty- to seventy-voice mixed choir, London Voices, a boys' choir of fifty, the London Oratory

School Schola, and then many folk soloists and instrumentalists from different parts of the compass. So it was a vast project but while I was doing the recording, Peter was always there, offering guidance and support, and showing you the crescendo that could go further, the dynamic that could be increased or lowered, the use of single instruments or soloists in very specific ways to add contrast, the use of silence – all of those things were done in a lot of detail, and in collaboration between Peter and myself.'

Jackson had wanted the films to transport the audience to another world, an ambition he undeniably achieved, and he credits Shore's music as playing a big part in helping him reach that goal. Mindful that the composer worked full-time on the trilogy, apart from providing two scores for regular collaborators David Fincher (*Panic Room*) and David Cronenberg (*Spider*), Jackson acknowledges that he and Walsh 'couldn't have actually wished for anything better. Howard has given us his total commitment and his heart and soul ... There has never been anything that's been too much trouble. He has worked himself into the ground, until the point of exhaustion, to put his best into this music and I totally admire and have great gratitude for him doing that.' Shore has since returned to this trilogy to rebuild the scores into a six-movement work for orchestra and choir, *The Lord of the Rings Symphony*, which has been performed live to sell-out crowds across the globe.

~

It was nearly a decade before Howard Shore and Peter Jackson would return to Middle-earth, so before focusing on the *Hobbit* trilogy it is instructive to explore the composer's long-standing partnerships with other directors, starting with David Cronenberg. They have worked on an impressive fifteen films together, from *The Brood* in 1979 to *Maps to the Stars* in 2014. Many scores are consciously uncomfortable to suit the subject matter – the director may be best known for his contribution to the 'body horror' canon – but musical recommendations are plentiful. *Eastern Promises* (2007), featuring guest soloist Nicola Benedetti, and *A Dangerous Method* (2011), with its Wagnerian influence, are great places to start, and the more adventurous should seek out *Naked Lunch*, which boasts a superb contribution from acclaimed jazz musician Ornette Coleman. There is clearly a lot of trust between Shore and Cronenberg, stemming from a rapport built up over the decades, and the two artists seem to work in tandem. The composer's affection for the director is clear: 'I've worked with David Cronenberg for thirty years, but each film grew into the next, and we tried many different ways of using music in film, many different techniques, and David was very adventurous and allowed me a lot of creative freedom. It was joyful, really, to work with him.'

Shore has collaborated with Martin Scorsese on six films over three decades, including *The Aviator* (2004), *The Departed* (2006) and *Hugo* (2011), and the working process is different, but equally fulfilling: 'Marty has a great mind for music. He has a vast collection of recordings in his archive. It's one of the great fun things of working with him and Thelma Schoonmaker, the great editor that he's worked with for many years, is that there is so much information being exchanged in the meetings, in the discussion of the film – we'll discuss other films, other pieces of music and it's just a very creative process to making movies.' It's interesting that, as with Jackson, this is not a clear-cut director–composer partnership but that there are other strong contributors. As Shore remarks, 'When you work with Marty and Thelma, you're on a journey to discover the story, find what works best for the film. You know, it's a lot of work, but it's really a period of discovery.'

According to Shore, the secret to building a strong composer–director relationship is: 'You need to grow. I think that's a very important part of working with a director over different films.' Looking back over his career, and what drove him personally, he says, 'My interest in film was in music and how I could express ideas using live musicians, live recording, but also working with electronics and working with the recording studio as an instrument itself. So it's important to allow the creative energy to flow, and as the years advance to keep creating new works. Not looking back, but always forward.'

When he considers the power structure between director and composer, Shore maintains that it's all about balance: 'The best relationships are the ones where there's a meeting of minds, where the ideas are presented and respected and the work is always creative. You can present your ideas in the most open way. Things can be adjusted here and there.'

❧

Jackson and Shore returned to Middle-earth for *An Unexpected Journey* (2012), *The Desolation of Smaug* (2013) and *The Battle of Five Armies* (2014), but it's worth noting that shortly after *The Lord of the Rings* they also worked together on Jackson's passion project, a remake of his beloved *King Kong* (2005). The director had been working on this before *The Lord of the Rings* but Universal Pictures cancelled production in 1997, partly due to the release of similar films around that time, such as *Godzilla* and *Mighty Joe Young*. After the success of his Middle-earth trilogy, Jackson was in demand, and chose to return to the Kong. He brought along most of his trusted crew from *The Lord of the Rings*, including Shore, and so it was quite a shock when they announced they were parting company a mere seven weeks before the premiere. Shore was replaced by James Newton Howard, and Jackson's official statement offered this by way of explanation: 'During the last few weeks, Howard and I came to real-ise that we had differing creative aspirations for the score of *King Kong*. Rather than waste time arguing with a friend and trying to unify our points of view, we decided amicably to let another composer score the film. I'm looking forward to working with James Newton Howard, a composer whose work I've long admired, and I thank Howard Shore, whose talent is surpassed only by his graciousness.'

This raises an important point when it comes to creative collabora-tions: just because some projects are conducive for two individuals, there is no guarantee that all will be. We can only speculate about the exact creative differences. Jackson may have been less amenable to sharing ideas because *King Kong* was such a personal project for him, or perhaps the pressures of the production were a contributing factor, considering its scale rivalled *The Lord of the Rings* – in fact, more visual effects were cre-ated for this film than for the entire trilogy. Early in his career, Jackson spoke of wanting 'total control of every aspect' of his films, and this has been corroborated by crew members: a production designer on *The Lord of the Rings* described the director as 'the last word' because designs had to be run past him. Only after receiving the thumbs-up from him – a message stating 'P.J. approved' – could they proceed.

Whatever Jackson's working methods, it would have been unthink-able for the *Hobbit* films to be scored by anyone other than Shore, considering the vast and multifaceted sound world he'd constructed for *The Lord of the Rings*. When the films were announced in 2007, origin-ally as a two-part series, Jackson was involved as co-writer and producer, but Guillermo del Toro was hired as director. The two worked closely on pre-production for two years but, by 2010, when the films had still not been officially green-lit, del Toro left the project due to the long production delay, and Jackson was a natural choice to replace him. The production schedule was not adjusted to allow for the replacement director to fully get behind the wheel so he was, in effect, chasing his tail from day one. Compare this to *The Lord of the Rings*, for which Jackson, Walsh and Boyens had had years of pre-production and the luxury of time to explore details, plot devices and characterisation. A noted perfectionist with a reputation for his attention to detail, known for taking days to shoot single scenes, it cannot have been an easy experience for Jackson. Filming started in March 2011 and continued through to July 2012, with two breaks of a month or two in between, allowing the cast and crew to get their breath back while Jackson and a small team recced new locations.

Shore devoted three more years to Tolkien, adding well over sixty more leitmotifs and reprising and recrafting earlier themes to create thematic 'families' for, for example, dwarves, hobbits and elves. 'It's really a tangent to *The Lord of the Rings*,' the composer explained in 2017, 'and it's a story that Tolkien created for his children. It's a much lighter story.' These light tones are evident in stand-out pieces 'Old Friends' and 'The World is Ahead', and his aim was to start off with these, then allow the music to become darker as the trilogy progresses, leaving the audience in the right musical environment for *The Lord of the Rings* and keeping things seamless in case fans chose to watch all six in succession. Even though Shore had reams of music as a starting-off point, the trilogy still required extreme commitment: 'We took our love of *The Lord of the Rings* and we infused it into *The Hobbit* because we loved the story, and we used our best techniques from the *Ring* story and developed that further in terms of themes and motifs.'

As with the first trilogy, even if the director and composer weren't in the same room, or on the same continent, there was regular communication. When recording the first *Hobbit* film, Shore would call Jackson while the orchestra was on a break to play him the short sections that had been recorded that day, and the director welcomed these pieces because they often influenced his creative process – music and film each informed the other. A busy schedule did not allow for Jackson to spend time in London, so recording for the second and third films was relocated to the Wellington Town Hall, with the New Zealand Symphony Orchestra recruited to perform. Despite reported time constraints on the production of the final film, the composer still managed to create new themes for *The Battle of Five Armies*, and for developed characters like Bain and Bolg, and the score contains treasures and surprises. 'Courage and Wisdom' and 'There and Back Again' instantly transport the audience back to Middle-earth, yet still feel fresh. Shore has said he had become so disciplined in his composition process for these films, and so open to his musical universe, that he still had more music to write, but had to drag himself away.

⌒⌇

The collaboration between Shore and Jackson is founded in a shared vision, mutual respect and a focused faith in the original text, which the director described as 'not just a book, but a whole mythic philosophy'. What sets their creative partnership apart from the others examined here is the inclusion of other key individuals on an equal footing with the director and composer, namely fellow screenwriters and producers Fran Walsh and Philippa Boyens. Shore and Jackson both put in the lion's share but such a huge project could never simply be a job for only two people, and with the support of additional collaborators the composer was able – for want of a better expression – to 'think big'. He has said that *The Lord of the Rings* 'completely changed the way I work'; in turn Jackson credits Shore for teaching him more about the scoring process, and that not only did he learn about instrumentation but 'I've also learned a lot about patience, he's one of the most patient people I've ever met.' But perhaps the strongest bond between them, in Jackson's eyes at least, was their joint devotion to the source material: 'It's a wonderful thing in a professional relationship to move beyond work into a friendship. That's the product of who he is and the time that we spent together. What I ultimately appreciate most about what Howard has done for us, which is separate to the music, is the fact that he has become as obsessed with Tolkien and *The Lord of the Rings* as Fran and I have.'

 ## Collaboration History

*The Lord of the Rings: The Fellowship of the Ring* (2001)
*The Lord of the Rings: The Two Towers* (2002)
*The Lord of the Rings: The Return of the King* (2003)
*The Hobbit: An Unexpected Journey* (2012)
*The Hobbit: The Desolation of Smaug* (2013)
*The Hobbit: The Battle of the Five Armies* (2014)

 ## Suggested Playlist

*The Lord of the Rings: The Fellowship of the Ring*, Concerning Hobbits
*The Lord of the Rings: The Fellowship of the Ring*, The Council of Elrond
*The Lord of the Rings: The Fellowship of the Ring*, Many Meetings
*The Lord of the Rings: The Fellowship of the Ring*, The Breaking of the Fellowship
*The Lord of the Rings: The Two Towers*, The Riders of Rohan
*The Lord of the Rings: The Two Towers*, The White Rider
*The Lord of the Rings: The Two Towers*, Forth Eolingas

*The Lord of the Rings: The Return of the King*, The Lighting of the Beacons

*The Lord of the Rings: The Return of the King*, The White Tree

*The Lord of the Rings: The Return of the King*, Twilight and Shadow

*The Lord of the Rings: The Return of the King*, The Return of the King

*The Hobbit: An Unexpected Journey*, Old Friends

*The Hobbit: An Unexpected Journey*, An Unexpected Party

*The Hobbit: An Unexpected Journey*, The World is Ahead

*The Hobbit: The Desolation of Smaug*, The Quest for Erebor

*The Hobbit: The Desolation of Smaug*, Feast of Starlight

*The Hobbit: The Battle of the Five Armies*, The Ruins of Dale

*The Hobbit: The Battle of the Five Armies*, Courage and Wisdom

*The Hobbit: The Battle of the Five Armies*, There and Back Again

# 10

# ALAN SILVESTRI AND ROBERT ZEMECKIS

*'The captain and the trusted crew'*

*I*f we measure the director–composer collaborations in this book solely by number, Robert Zemeckis and Alan Silvestri, who have worked on sixteen films together, are hot on the heels of Steven Spielberg and John Williams in terms of pedigree. Since their first collaboration in 1984, *Romancing the Stone*, Zemeckis has chosen Silvestri to score every single one of his movies, from the *Back to the Future* trilogy to the wartime spy drama *Allied* in 2016. These films hop across genres but whether they're suspense, children's movies or black comedy, each has a sense of playfulness and a sheer joy in their craft that have propelled both director and composer from big-budget blockbusters and award successes, such as *Forrest Gump*, to more serious drama in later years, such as *Flight*. There is an unashamedly broad appeal to the Zemeckis–Silvestri partnership, which has provided entertainment and escapism for many households across the decades. If you don't have fond memories of watching and rewatching, say, *Who Framed Roger Rabbit* on VHS, or *The Polar Express* on DVD, more's the pity.

As with many of the collaborations featured in this book, while the director hasn't, to date, worked with any other composer, you can't say the same for the composer. Alan Silvestri's remarkable back catalogue incorporates superhero fare (the *Avengers* series), animation (*Lilo & Stitch* and *The Croods*) and action and sci-fi (*Predator* and *The Abyss*). He's worked on three projects with director Stephen Sommers, including *The Mummy Returns*, and on all of the *Night at the Museum* films, directed by Shawn Levy. He has also collaborated with other notable directors including Sam Raimi, Gore Verbinski and even Steven Spielberg, in a rare project scored by someone other than John Williams, 2018's *Ready Player One*. For those of a certain vintage, there's a strong chance Silvestri soundtracked your formative film viewing in the 1980s or 1990s, with films including *Flight of the Navigator*, *Father of the Bride*, *Overboard* and *The Parent Trap*.

⤛

Alan Silvestri spent a few years at Berklee College of Music and had a brief spell as a drummer in a rock band called The Herd, formed in his hometown of Teaneck, New Jersey. His first scoring project was the low-budget film *The Dobermans* in 1972. He did most of his musical groundwork in television, including *Starsky & Hutch* and crime drama *CHiPs*, for which he was the main composer from 1977 to 1983. He has continued to contribute to the small screen throughout his career, teaming up with Robert Zemeckis on episodes of *Amazing Stories* and *Tales from the Crypt*, and he won two Emmy Awards in 2014 for his music for the science documentary series *Cosmos: A Spacetime Odyssey*. When he met Robert Zemeckis in 1983 he was still learning his craft, with regular

TV work and several films under his belt, and was on the lookout for a project he could really sink his teeth into.

Robert Zemeckis spent a large portion of his youth watching television and going to the movies. He can recall the first film he ever saw – *The Blob* – and quickly progressed from a young film fan to an aspiring film-maker: 'I was fascinated by the illusion of the movies before anything else. I was always trying to figure out how they did something, like a visual effect, or how they did an action sequence, and I became obsessed with how they synched sound up with the picture. I tried to do that with home movies. So I guess my passion for film came from the technical end first.'

He studied film at the University of Southern California, where he met his early writing collaborator, Bob Gale. After winning a Student Academy Award at USC for a short film called *Field of Honor*, he found himself face-to-face with Steven Spielberg, who became a mentor to the aspiring director and executive produced his first two films, *I Wanna Hold Your Hand* (1978) and *Used Cars* (1980). Both received some critical praise but didn't fare well at the box office. Zemeckis and Gale then provided the screenplay for the Spielberg war romp *1941,* which turned out to be an uncharacteristic flop for the director of *Jaws* and *Close Encounters of the Third Kind*. So, during the early 1980s, Zemeckis was feeling the need to prove himself. He and Gale continued writing, and pitched their idea of a teenager who accidentally travels back in time to the 1950s but it was turned down by the major studios.

Steven Spielberg would go on to executive produce the *Back to the Future* trilogy and *Who Framed Roger Rabbit* but at this stage, in 1983, Zemeckis was keen to find his own feet as a director. As luck would have it, Michael Douglas hired him to direct **Romancing the Stone**. Studio executives were expecting a flop and many critics dismissed it as a *Raiders* *of the Lost Ark* rip-off – despite the fact the screenplay had actually been written before the first *Indiana Jones* film – but it was a box-office hit, providing Zemeckis with the clout to get his time-travelling tale into production. A definitive turning point in his career, and also his first encounter with Alan Silvestri.

By his own admission, Zemeckis hadn't concerned himself too much with the matter of who to hire to score *Romancing the Stone* before Silvestri, keen for the challenge of scoring an adventure film that would require a range of styles, from action cues to love themes, walked into his office and played him his audition tape. Despite Silvestri not having seen footage of the film, the composer's music felt instinctively connected to the story, and the director, whose initial impression was of 'a good guy who laughed and smiled easily, just a solid human being', signed him up. The resulting score brings the romcom elements to the forefront with jazzy elements like the jolly saxophone providing the centrepiece to the end titles, creating an atmosphere of light-hearted warmth.

⁓

Perhaps not even Robert Zemeckis and Bob Gale themselves could have anticipated the success of ***Back to the Future***. It was the highest-grossing film of 1985, spawning two sequels and receiving four Academy Award nominations – including one for Zemeckis and Gale for Best Original Screenplay – and it won the Oscar for Best Sound Effects Editing. Few films have made as much of a mark in our collective psyches or continue to feature in 'must-see movies' lists, and fewer still have been quoted by the American president in their State of the Union Address, as was the case with Ronald Reagan in 1986 when he quoted Doc Brown's famous line: 'Where we're going, we don't need roads.'

The idea for *Back to the Future* came about when Gale was looking through his father's high-school yearbook and wondered whether he would have been friends with his teenage dad. In the original film, Marty McFly travels back to 1955 to ensure his parents fall in love – fending off his mother's romantic advances in the process – and in *Back to the Future Part II* he and Doc head to a futuristic 2015 to save his children from going to prison. Picking up where the first film left off, it builds on intertwining timelines that the third film (shot at the same time as *Part II* and released the year after it, in 1990) expands on, bringing the action to 1885 before returning to 1985. By weaving the timelines together, the trilogy becomes a cohesive whole, unlike many sequels that can feel tacked on to the original.

Silvestri's main theme for *Back to the Future* is everything you'd expect and hope for: big, dramatic and exciting, it stands squarely in the hit movie-music canon alongside John Williams hits such as *Raiders of the Lost Ark* and *Superman*. In 2016, Silvestri explained how it evolved out of a visit he made to the set when they were filming the 'Enchantment Under the Sea' high-school dance, a key scene from the 1955 part of the movie in which George and Lorraine, later to be Marty's parents, share their first kiss: 'They were shooting it in a church in Los Angeles, and it was probably the busiest day of the entire shoot because of the sheer number of extras and people involved . . . We didn't have much time to talk about the film but [Zemeckis] turned to me at one point and he raised his hands over his head, and he said, "Al, it's gotta be *big*!"'

Silvestri continued, 'As I started to work through the film, I [began] to understand what he was communicating. I think a large part of that was, he really didn't have any big shots in the film, he didn't have big vistas, shots of the desert and mountain ranges that went for miles and miles. Everything was small, image-wise, in the film: it was the town square, it was the McFly house, and yet the story was a story of heroism and great friendship and great love.'

Silvestri set to work on a theme that would embody such grand ideals. Perhaps surprisingly, as he explains, what he came up with could also be described as 'just as a tune. It literally is as you would write a song – it's got a verse, it's got a release and kind of a pay-off-type chorus.' In all its glory, played by over a hundred musicians, it went down wonderfully well with Zemeckis. Audiences similarly took the main theme to their hearts and elements were subsequently incorporated into the sequels, such as the *Back to the Future III* end titles. Silvestri went into composing the scores for the two follow-up films knowing he had received the seal of approval with his music for the original film but also aware of the weight of audience expectation when it came to reusing and reworking now-familiar motifs.

He equates the concept of a sequel to having old friends – as well as enemies, which as he points out are an equally important asset in a sequel to a successful film. Along with those existing characters, in which we are already invested, there are other aspects of the film that feel familiar to us, such as the way it is shot or, of course, the music; these became part of the 'paint box', as he put it, that he and Zemeckis and other members of the crew worked with to create the next film.

'Because the sequels will move into new narrative areas, new relation-ships and all kinds of things, you're going to need some more paints than just the ones that were developed in the original film, but you keep all of the ones that were in the original there alongside them, to be used whenever it's appropriate . . . We knew that this *Back to the Future* theme resonated with our audience, and that was an amazing thing to have going into *Back to the Future Part II* and *Part III* . . . It equates to a kind of freedom because you already have things there that you know will work and will pay off, which you didn't know when you began the first film.'

❧

Between the release of the original *Back to the Future* film and its sequels, Zemeckis embarked on another adventurous project, this time merging animation with live action in **Who Framed Roger Rabbit**. Released in 1988, at the time it was the most expensive animated film ever to be green-lit, and as with so many movies, the end result could have been very different if the studio's first choices had accepted the offer. Apparently Disney asked Monty Python star Terry Gilliam to direct but he declined, while Harrison Ford, Bill Murray and Eddie Murphy had all been considered for the role of Eddie Valiant, which eventually went to Bob Hoskins.

It's hard now to think of anyone else fulfilling the part of the jaded private detective as well as Hoskins, and it's equally tough to imagine any director other than Robert Zemeckis at the helm of this technically challenging project. He created a visual treat that is, in itself, a celebration of film-making, with knowing nods to and heartfelt nostalgia about Hollywood's Golden Age. Silvestri composed an evocative score to fit the 1940s setting, with the piano swirls of 'Eddie's Theme' instantly conjuring up images of smoky jazz clubs. He clearly relished the task of creating a musical homage to the era: 'Valiant & Valiant' opens with a slower, melancholic version of the refrain from 'Eddie's Theme' before perking up halfway through with the help of a double bass.

The versatile composer sounds as if he's having just as much fun in **Death Becomes Her** (1992), from the knowing strings at the start of the 'Main Title' that entice the audience with horror tropes before welcoming in light orchestral tones, setting the scene for the black comedy ahead. The end credits offer an extended version of this theme, reminiscent both of the suspense of Bernard Herrmann and the playfulness of Danny Elfman, with an atmosphere that is gleeful, tense and magical.

The story of two feuding women who drink a potion for eternal youth was another opportunity for Zemeckis to experiment with his passion for visual trickery, and it's hard to forget the image of Meryl Streep with her head twisted all the way around, embracing Bruce Willis who's holding a candlestick with a hand that just so happens to go through a hole in Goldie Hawn's stomach. *Death Becomes Her* was Zemeckis' first leap into the world of computer imagery and he sees it as the next step in a career that has embraced complexity: 'Every movie I've done so far is more complicated than the one previous. I don't know if that's a good trend or not.' The film was another commercial success and it won the Academy Award for Best Visual Effects, but it was his next directorial project that would cement his reputation as a world-class storyteller.

❧

The tale of a slow but warm-hearted man who indirectly or unintentionally affects various historical events, and his enduring love for his childhood friend Jenny, *Forrest Gump* (1994) picked up six Oscars in total, including Best Picture, Best Actor for Tom Hanks, and Best Director. Zemeckis puts the achievement down to teamwork and a shared goal, stating, 'I was able to do good things in *Forrest Gump* because everybody was always ready and prepared and willing to work.' The film earned Silvestri his first nomination for Best Original Score – his only nod in that category to date – though his music is far less overt than in Zemeckis' earlier films. Pop and rock hits from the era by the likes of Elvis Presley, the Doors and Lynyrd Skynyrd soundtrack many key moments within the film, but it is Silvestri's music that underpins the more emotional elements in the story. Crucially for him it was a lesson in restraint, and a significant example of an occasion when he disagreed with a director.

Robert Zemeckis and Alan Silvestri during a scoring
session for *A Christmas Carol*, 2009.

'There was a moment in *Forrest Gump* where Jenny leaves the house
early in the morning and doesn't say goodbye to Forrest. She just leaves
him there. Bob shows this cut of Forrest looking into her bedroom from
the door with this look on this face as though he knows something has
happened here, and then there's this shot of Forrest sitting in the window
seat . . . [with a] long camera move. And when we sat and spotted the
film, discussed the film, I didn't want to play any music for this. I remember Bob turned to me and said, "Really? You're not hearing anything
here, Al?" – which is the way he always refers to it . . . This is the kind
of sequence that I would say could make a director very nervous about
being this exposed, with no music, and there couldn't be any effects, so
it was basically a silent camera move. I said, "Bob, if you want me to play
something, of course, I will always do that, but if you're asking me, then
no, I think it shouldn't have music."'

For Zemeckis, it was an example of how well their relationship worked that Silvestri could say that to him: 'That is like gold – because you don't have any objectivity any more.' Zemeckis acknowledges what must be a common experience: becoming too close to the material you're working on and consequently feeling unable to tell for sure whether a particular scene is working – at which point it is tempting to want to 'shore it up with music'. But sometimes the composer's job is to advocate no music as the better option, as it ultimately proved in this case.

They came to a compromise by allowing the audience to decide at an early test screening of a 'work-in-progress' version of the film. According to Silvestri, Zemeckis reserved the right to come back to him to ask for music if the audience didn't respond favourably to the scene. At the end of a rapt viewing, he turned to Silvestri and said, 'OK, no music', and that was that.

Weighing up both sides of the creative argument is important for Silvestri. Ultimately he sees his responsibility as speaking up if he feels strongly about something but accepting that a final decision is the director's prerogative. 'I don't always fall on my sword, I feel I owe it to him to bring my sensibility and my impressions and all the rest of it, and if for whatever reason he feels there's a different approach, then I will always do what he asks because he is the captain, and he does have a perspective on this film that truly no one else in the entire creative process has, and that has to be respected.'

⁓

From the mid 1990s and into the next decade, both composer and director enjoyed playing with different genres, such as Silvestri's Herrmannesque score for Zemeckis' unashamedly Hitchcockian thriller *What Lies Beneath* (2000). This was shot back-to-back with *Cast Away* (2001), or to be precise, it was made in between: the crew shot the first part of *Cast Away*, made *What Lies Beneath* to give Tom Hanks time to lose weight and grow a beard, then returned to the tale of the man stranded on an island. Apparently Zemeckis had flagged up this interesting dual production process to Silvestri in 1998, asking him to set aside the year 2000 to score both films, to build suspense with one project and create emotional isolation with the other. Previously, Silvestri had made a worthy contribution to the sci-fi movie-music canon with **Contact** (1997), Zemeckis' project directly after *Forrest Gump*, in which he soundtracked the story of scientists trying to communicate with extra-terrestrial life with real delicacy. The gentle 'I Believe Her' is a great example of his versatility and the score is one of his finest, subtle and nuanced, and the perfect accompaniment to the film's wider themes of humanity and discovery.

Unsurprisingly for a director who has said, 'I just hope my body of work is always one of stretching. I don't ever want to go back over any familiar territory', Zemeckis has continued to experiment with new visual effects and technologies, in particular performance-capture techniques, a type of animation created from the recorded motions of the actors, as used in *Beowulf* (2007), *A Christmas Carol* (2009) and, most significantly, **The Polar Express** (2004), which was listed in the *Guinness World Book of Records* as the first all-digital capture film. It also earned Silvestri his second Oscar nomination for 'Believe', co-written with Glen Ballard and in the running for Best Original Song, although a more memorable musical moment for many is the energetic 'Hot Chocolate' sung by regular Zemeckis collaborator Tom Hanks as the conductor of the magical train.

≈

Considering the variety of films the director and composer had worked on by the mid 2000s, it's worth taking a moment to explore how they approach each project, and whether they have found a set pattern that they adhere to in order to achieve the most effective results.

Silvestri describes their creative process as follows: 'If there is something to read, he'll send it to me, and we'll have an initial phone chat, maybe a dinner, talking about the movie ... I pretty much never see anything while they're shooting, I don't look at dailies, I don't see a scene here or there. And then when he first sees the assembly of the film, I sit with him and watch the film as a film, even though he for the most part hasn't started to work on it, editorial-wise, himself. And that's an amazing event because I get to see the raw material of the film.

'And then he goes off and does his director's cut, and when he's got through that process for the first time, we go through the traditional spotting session where we start with the first frame of the film, and we stop and go all the way through ... We discuss every scene in detail, where music will begin, where it will end, where there should be music, where there shouldn't be, what we think the tone should be ... And then I go off and I start to write, and then, as things appear, I send them to him and he gives me his notes, and we start to creatively work, piece of music by piece of music, all the way through the film.'

Over the decades, the two have developed an intuitive way of working, as Zemeckis explained in 2000: 'You develop a shorthand. You know how the person is thinking or feeling. I'm sure Al can sense how I feel about a cue when I say the first word or by the look on my face.'

These early discussions provide an invaluable steer to the composer, but not necessarily because they offer clarity. Silvestri has previously described Zemeckis as *not* specific in his musical directions and explains that he, the composer, finds such an open approach powerful: 'He's very interested in having someone bring their perspective to him, and so he's very open about my impressions of his film. He invites all of us who work with him to bring something to him. That being said, he very clearly understands his film and knows, certainly as you go through the process, what it needs . . . So when I say he's not specific it's only in the most initial phase where he lets the film speak for itself to see what his creative team will find and what they will bring in response to that.'

☙

In the 2010s, Zemeckis–Silvestri films have inclined towards more character-driven stories with *Flight* (2012), the story of a pilot who crash-lands a plane and is hailed a hero until it is revealed he was intoxicated during the flight; *The Walk* (2015), a warm-hearted biographical drama about Philippe Petit's high-wire walk between the Twin Towers in 1974; and *Allied* (2016). The Second World War romantic thriller received mixed reviews, overshadowed in the press by news of star Brad Pitt's divorce and the surrounding rumours, but the music shows yet another dimension to the composer. The soundtrack features eight Silvestri cues along with a selection of existing swing and jazz numbers and he manages to create an atmosphere of portent in the muted 'Main Title', alongside tender moments such as 'It's a Girl'.

Their sixteenth collaboration serves as a reminder that despite decades of working together, it's not all plain sailing. Creative differences do, and did, arise. On this occasion, Silvestri watched raw film footage with Zemeckis before the director had started cutting, and the composer decided to get started on a piece of music to fit a long sequence at the end that he felt was the heart of the film. After working on it for a few weeks, he sent a presentation over to Zemeckis. It was a difficult time for Silvestri, whose father died while he was working on this composition, and Zemeckis was aware of his creative partner's loss, as Silvestri explained: 'The phone rang on a Saturday morning, and Bob started to talk about my dad. We probably talked for forty-five minutes about our fathers – he had lost his father years ago – and at the end he said, "Look, I got this material you sent me, we don't have to talk about the movie now." And I said, "It's OK, this is what I've been doing, we should talk about it." He said, "OK, but I just want to let you know, it isn't going to be pretty. I think you're 180 degrees off on this." And then he proceeded to tell me why.'

Zemeckis values being able to speak frankly to the composer, and credits Silvestri for being receptive to feedback and not being too precious about his craft: 'What he taught me is that there's no mystery in it, it's definitely workable, and I should speak my mind. Most composers put up this wall of mystery around what it is they do. I wouldn't ever suggest anything musical to Al, but if I don't think something's working for the scene the way I had envisioned it, I will express that and he'll either listen, disagree, talk me out of it or go ahead and change it.'

In turn, Silvestri is receptive to feedback because he knows the director is being honest and constructive: 'The thing that's fantastic about Bob is that this is done with the utmost respect and love, but it is very clear. More than anything, he wants to give me what I need in terms of direction to do my work . . . Now this was a case where we hadn't spotted the movie, we hadn't sat and had discussions about it, I just went off on my own, but clearly he thought that the direction I had taken was 180 degrees off. And then he was eloquent in how he described why he felt that – and he was right!'

⤳

Over the decades, Silvestri and Zemeckis have collaborated on a vast array of projects and worked through any creative differences they encountered on the way, but more crucially they have become good friends. The director has referred to the composer as his 'creative soul-mate' and Silvestri compares their partnership to a marriage, noting that just as he and his wife don't always see eye to eye, in both relationships 'there is this underlying sense of a common goal and a common way of seeing that goal'. He notes the importance of compatibility but is generous about the director's role ultimately being paramount: 'Bob does not write music but needs music as part of his art, and we have somehow found our way to together accomplish his needs in his films and it's kind of a miracle!'

Zemeckis clearly recognises the value in having a strong team surrounding him, and has forged other long-term collaborations in his crew, such as editor Arthur Schmidt who worked on every film from *Back to the Future* to *Cast Away*, winning Oscars for Best Film Editing for *Who Framed Roger Rabbit* and *Forrest Gump*, or cinematographer Dean Cundey who was involved in six movies from *Romancing the Stone* to *Death Becomes Her*, a key player in paving the director's early success in the 1980s and early 1990s. All members of the crew need to understand how their contributions fit into the film, which then becomes more than the sum of its parts. Zemeckis values Silvestri for his ability to compose within that conception: 'He doesn't just write songs that call attention to themselves. His music always supports the images and the performances, it's that extra layer, and his approach to the music is always that we're making a movie here.'

Zemeckis has referred to himself as a general commandeering a large army on set, but the composer prefers a naval rather than military approach: 'I always refer to the ship analogy ... the director clearly is, and should be and must be, the captain of a ship. Everyone else on that ship is crew and my advice to anyone who wishes to have a long-standing relationship with a director is that that must never be forgotten because as that saying goes, "You're either part of the solution or you are part of the problem", and the director's job is to solve all of the problems for the film. As part of the director's trusted crew, I think the composer needs to solve the musical problems, but in doing so not unnecessarily add to the overwhelming burden that the director is already dealing with.'

Looking back, Silvestri says he was young and anxious when they first started working together around thirty-five years ago, and inevitably leaned on Zemeckis for reassurance. But over time he learned to manage his own needs without burdening the director – an essential requirement for a successful long-term collaboration, in his eyes. Once again, the marriage analogy is apt: 'As you spend more time with your partner – I think that's what falling more deeply in love has to do with – [you reach an] understanding where you're different and respect that in the person you're in the relationship with, and inflict less of yourself on them unnecessarily!'

His advice for anyone wanting to work with a director like Robert Zemeckis and build a similarly long and fruitful working relationship with them is to continue developing one's craft and be receptive to new creative challenges: 'They are not standing still artistically, they are constantly growing, constantly exploring, and if you are not doing that in your particular art, you will not, at some point, be invited to go along on the journey with them because you haven't grown. You must grow.'

##  Collaboration History

*Romancing the Stone* (1984)

*Back to the Future* (1985)

*Amazing Stories* (1985), television; episode: 'Go to the Head of the Class'

*Who Framed Roger Rabbit* (1988)

*Tales from the Crypt* (1989–96), television; selected episodes

*Back to the Future Part II* (1989)

*Back to the Future Part III* (1990)

*Death Becomes Her* (1992)

*Forrest Gump* (1994)

*Contact* (1997)

*What Lies Beneath* (2000)

*Cast Away* (2000)

*The Polar Express* (2004)

*Beowulf* (2007)

*A Christmas Carol* (2009)

*Flight* (2012)

*The Walk* (2015)

*Allied* (2016)

 ## Suggested Playlist

*Romancing the Stone*, End Titles

*Back to the Future*, Main Theme

*Who Framed Roger Rabbit*, Eddie's Theme

*Who Framed Roger Rabbit*, Valiant & Valiant

*Back to the Future Part II*, The Future

*Back to the Future Part III*, End Credits

*Death Becomes Her*, End Credits

*Forrest Gump*, I'm Forrest . . . Forrest Gump

*Forrest Gump*, Suite

*Contact*, I Believe Her

*Contact*, End Credits

*What Lies Beneath*, Forbidden Fruit

*Cast Away*, End Credits

*The Polar Express*, Hot Chocolate

*Beowulf*, What We Need Is a Hero

*The Walk*, Perhaps You Brought Them to Life – Given Them a Soul

*Allied*, Essaouira Desert/Main Title

*Allied*, It's a Girl

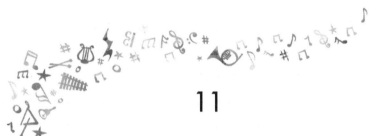

# 11

# JOHN WILLIAMS AND STEVEN SPIELBERG

*'A perfect association'*

'ithout question, John Williams has been the single most significant contributor to my success.' So said Steven Spielberg, the highest-grossing film director in history, at Williams' eightieth birthday gala in 2012.

In the world of composer–director partnerships, the collaboration between Williams and Spielberg is hands down the most seamless. They have worked together on a jaw-dropping twenty-eight films directed by Spielberg to date, creating some of the most memorable moments in cinema for more than four decades, from *Jaws* and *E.T.* to *Schindler's List* and *Jurassic Park*, through to *War Horse*, *Lincoln* and *The BFG*. Spielberg has said that 'John has transformed and uplifted every movie that we've made together' and it's far easier to list Spielberg's full-length directorial features that haven't been scored by Williams, as there are only three: *The Color Purple*, *Bridge of Spies* and most recently *Ready Player One* – which was handed over to Alan Silvestri because Williams was busy scoring their most recent collaboration, *The Post*.

The composer has described their partnership as a perfect marriage, and it's certainly a profitable pairing, resulting in box-office gold as well as the most enduring and hummable musical motifs. John Williams has a rare musical gift, bringing a film to life in his scores and adding an emotional connection between the audience and the story.

It was an auspicious relationship from the start, with Spielberg describing Williams as 'the only person that I've had a perfect association with' during their first decade of working together. For Williams' part, their collaboration has proved to be so fruitful not solely because they get on well but because of the respect they both place on a film's score, understanding the impetus it can give the narrative. In an interview from 1975, shortly after the success of *Jaws*, Williams said, 'The best directors are musical; I think part of what they do is musical. The art of editing film in my mind is a musical art.'

In 2016, when the American Film Institute presented John Williams with a Lifetime Achievement Award, the first time a composer has received that honour, Williams thanked Spielberg for having such good taste in his movie projects, as well as patience with him, while the director concluded his speech with a succinct reflection on Williams' contribution to film – not just to his own movies but to other hits, including *Star Wars*, *Superman* and the *Harry Potter* series, which have been elevated by the composer's magic touch: 'Without John Williams, bikes don't really fly, nor do brooms in Quidditch matches, nor do men in red capes. There is no Force, dinosaurs do not walk the Earth, we do not wonder, we do not weep, we do not believe.'

John Williams' career path was set from an early age. His father, Johnny Williams, was a drummer, performing in studio orchestras and jazz groups. Williams learned to read music when he was around five or six, and assumed he'd have a career as a pianist. In fact, his entry into the world of film studios was playing the piano on classic scores such as *To Kill a Mockingbird* by Elmer Bernstein, and he also conducted studio orchestras – sometimes including his own father. He moved into composing when he was asked to provide orchestrations of works by legends from the Golden Age of Hollywood who were still going strong: Alfred Newman, Franz Waxman, Dimitri Tiomkin and Bernard Herrmann, who later became a friend.

Williams soon established himself as a fine film composer, carving a niche in the disaster-movie genre with his music for *The Towering Inferno*, *Earthquake* and *The Poseidon Adventure*. He won his first Academy Award in the now defunct category of Best Scoring Adaptation and Original Song Score for *Fiddler on the Roof* in 1972, having received his first nomination in 1968 for *Valley of the Dolls*. He also formed an early fruitful collaboration with director Mark Rydell, with successes including *The Reivers* (1969) and *The Cowboys* (1972), both of which impressed a young Steven Spielberg.

Spielberg, whose mother was a concert pianist, collected film soundtracks from a young age. Movies were his passion, and after making a short western film on his father's movie camera in order to get his Boy Scout photography merit badge, he continued experimenting with film-making at home. At the age of sixteen, he wrote and directed his first independent film, *Firelight*, and when he was a student he got an unpaid internship at Universal Studios in the editing department. He made a short film, *Amblin'*, which won some awards and impressed the studio vice-president so much that he was offered a seven-year directing contract, making Spielberg the youngest director to receive such a commitment from a major studio. Television work followed, including an episode of *Columbo* and some TV movies such as *Duel*, but his first feature-length film for cinematic release was **The Sugarland Express** (1974).

Spielberg had spent so much time listening to Williams' earlier movie music that he wore out the LPs, and later admitted to having written a screenplay while listening to *The Reivers* 'because I found the score so inspirational'. Williams' music sounded like the Golden Age greats, so the young film-maker had assumed that the composer would be in his seventies or eighties, and he was pleasantly surprised to discover that John was only fifteen years older than him. Williams recalls meeting Spielberg at a glamorous Beverly Hills restaurant, as the director was keen to make a good impression, but his initial thoughts were also about age: the composer has described him as looking about seventeen years old, still at high school. As he said in 2012, however, he realised very quickly he was speaking to someone who knew a lot about movies and film music.

*The Sugarland Express* is a crime drama based on a real-life incident about a couple on the run from the law in a bid to prevent their son being put in foster care. Partially set in Sugar Land, Texas, Spielberg had envisaged a sweeping, American score, in a similar style to *The Reivers*. However, after watching the film, Williams had a different idea, and persuaded the director to consider the small-scale, human story, focusing on the couple rather than the expansive landscape. He suggested an intimate score performed by a small ensemble, and placed the film in Texas by incorporating harmonica solos, and the bluesy theme is a woozy, wistful treat.

The story of a shark terrorising a seaside resort was the defining moment in launching Steven Spielberg's career, and it was *Jaws* (1975) that cemented his collaboration with John Williams. The composer created such an iconic score with *those* repeated low notes that the director remarked in 2000, 'To this day, I think that his score was clearly responsible for half the success of the film.'

Williams has put the success of the film and his music down to our primal fear of monsters. The shark was the focus of his discussions with Spielberg about the score, as the director wanted a musical identifier for the creature. He watched the film in a projection room at Universal Studios, leaving the screening in a state of excitement to set about composing a deceptively simple score, with the aim of creating music that feels instinctive, just as a shark moves instinctively – in effect, making a character out of music.

It's well documented that the making of *Jaws* was fraught. The project nearly never reached cinemas because the estimated budget was soon vastly exceeded, the scheduled 55-day production ran past 150 days, and there were plenty of technical and logistical problems – not least the shark itself. Named Bruce after Spielberg's lawyer, the mechanical shark sank when it first entered the water. It was such an unreliable device that the director needed alternatives, and the problem was eventually solved by including point-of-view shots from the shark's perspective, which were then given extra impact by the music.

Spielberg initially thought Williams was joking when he played him the now famous notes on the piano: 'At first I began to laugh, and I thought, "John has a great sense of humour!" But he was serious – that was the theme for *Jaws*. So he played it again and again, and suddenly it seemed right. Sometimes the best ideas are the most simple ones and John had found a signature for the entire score.' Williams convinced Spielberg that the cellos and basses in the orchestra would make the music menacing, and explained that the effect of quickening the repeated notes and building the volume would increase a sense of panic. The bass ostinato – the repetition of two notes – and the unexpected introduction of a third note is as central to cinema as Herrmann's strings in the *Psycho* shower scene. When Williams conducts the *Jaws* theme in concert, he says the audience recognise it from the very first note – and that their reaction is often to giggle, somewhat surprisingly, perhaps due to its ubiquity or the incongruity of hearing a horror film theme in a classical concert setting.

But there's more to the score than the shark motif, and the composer is fond of his music for the barrel chase sequence: 'Suddenly, as the shark overpowers them and eventually escapes, the music deflates and ends with a little sea shanty called "Spanish Lady". The score musically illustrates and punctuates all of this dramatic outline.' Jaunty jigs represent the seasoned shark-hunter Quint, and these fit well with high-spirited elements that are reminiscent of pirate scores from the 1930s by the likes of Erich Wolfgang Korngold.

John Williams won a BAFTA, a Golden Globe, a Grammy and an Oscar for his score for *Jaws*, and the film was a staggering box-office success. It was the highest-grossing movie of all time – a title it held for a couple of years until the release of *Star Wars* – and made Spielberg one of the youngest multi-millionaires in America.

⮑

The director and composer were planning their third collaboration, ***Close Encounters of the Third Kind*** (1977), before the second was complete. Spielberg, who had written this story of aliens communicating with humans, recalls 'even before he wrote the score for *Jaws*, we were having meetings about *Close Encounters*'. Music was even more vital to this film because the two life forms use it to speak to each other, and as the signature theme needed to be played on-set by the actors, Williams was required to work on this score before he had finished yet another project, *Star Wars*. He used atonal orchestral effects to help place the UFOs in their ordinary settings on earth, and in 1978 compared the two sci-fi scores: '*Close Encounters* is more atmospheric and impressionistic; more abstract; and certainly less romantic than *Star Wars*.'

It is a consciously disorienting score. Many of the special effects were put on in post-production, and there was a lot of back and forth between the effects team and the editors, so there was no finished film for Williams to work from. As a result, he is said to have used a lot of 'blind-writing' techniques when composing sequences, taking inspiration from sketches or descriptions from Spielberg. The main task was to create a memorable musical message between scientists and aliens – a conversation between the two. The composer wrote a five-note motif, although he was originally keen to use seven notes so that it would fit with 'When You Wish Upon a Star' from *Pinocchio*, which is referenced early in the film and had been the film's original end titles. However Spielberg was keen for five notes, so it sounded more like a greeting, or a signal, and their next challenge was to decide which notes to use.

Speaking to *Film and Filming* magazine in 1978, Williams recalled: 'I wrote about two hundred motifs; you know, just sat down at the piano and figured out examples for him. We started to get confused, because one sounded better than another, this one was more melodic, that one was better as a signal, etc. Steven asked a mathematics friend how many combinations were possible within the twelve-note scale and found out it was something like 134,000! So I'd hardly scratched the surface with my two hundred!'

They kept returning to one particular sequence that ends on the fifth note of the diatonic scale, known as the dominant, and a musical formation that the composer compares to 'ending a sentence with the word "and"'. Such an ambiguous structure is significant in a film that explores possibilities and interactions with other life forms: the sequence can be repeated on loop, the music can move into something new or simply end, leaving the listener hanging.

❧

Everyone's favourite adventurous archaeologist, Indiana Jones, is set to return to the big screen in 2020, which will mark Spielberg's and Williams' twenty-ninth collaboration as composer and director, and it will be a welcome return for one of the composer's best-loved marches. That's high praise when you consider the 'Imperial March' from *The Empire Strikes Back* or his often overlooked but brilliant 'March' from a rare Spielberg misfire, *1941*. But the 'Raiders March' from Indy's first outing, **Raiders of the Lost Ark** (1981), is near perfection, paying homage to adventure films from the 1930s with a feel-good sincerity. The key to the Indiana Jones scores, as intended by creator George Lucas, is that they are celebrations – not send-ups – of matinee romps with feats of derring-do that were so popular decades before.

Williams is typically modest about the 'Raiders March', admitting it was a struggle at first. In the short film *The Music of Indiana Jones*, directed by their go-to documentary maker Laurent Bouzereau, the composer confesses he spends a huge amount of time working through all possible permutations of the most simple motifs, to ensure he has exactly the right notes and can make those tunes seem 'inevitable', explaining that the 'little simplicities are the hardest things to capture'. He composed two possible themes and played them to Spielberg, who claims his only input was to ask, 'Can't you use them both?' – which he did. Williams credits the comedy and swagger of Harrison Ford's performance for assisting in his composition process while Ford, in turn, told us he has been 'blessed by the scale of talent of John Williams' in his iconic screen roles as both Indy and Han Solo: 'I am often introduced with John Williams' music to accompany me, which is not a bad thing to have happen!'

The 'Raiders March' features the sweeping and romantic 'Marion's Theme', another stand-out cue from the first film, but as Ford pointed out in his speech to mark Williams' Lifetime Achievement Award at the AFI in 2016, this theme does not represent Marion herself but rather Indy's feelings for her. It does not appear when he meets her in a bar, but when a car blows up and he thinks she is dead, encouraging the audience to be aware of the hero's sense of loss – a great example of how Williams uses music to reinforce the emotional connection between audience and film.

The next film in the series, *Indiana Jones and the Temple of Doom* (1984), was darker in tone than *Raiders of the Lost Ark* and the music reflects that, with overpowering choruses during scenes in the temple, and represents the north Indian setting with instruments such as sitars and tabla drums. Spielberg is particularly fond of the trek music as Indy and his gang move across the country on elephants. Williams composed a more tender, at times melancholy, score for *Indiana Jones and the Last Crusade* (1989) to focus on the father–son relationship between Indiana and Henry Jones Sr. In *The Music of Indiana Jones*, Spielberg says it's his favourite of the three scores due to the evocation of that relationship, but there are also energetic moments within the music, such as the opening scene with a teenage Indy involving snakes on a train and a later chase, fittingly called 'Scherzo for Motorcycle and Orchestra'.

The three original Indiana Jones films are considered a near-faultless trilogy, so it was somewhat surprising to learn that a new instalment was on the horizon for 2008, breaking a nineteen-year absence from the big screen. Spielberg was keen to do another adventure-friendly film for all the family, something he hadn't done since *Jurassic Park* in 1993, and Williams likened the experience of returning to his earlier scores in his preparation for *Indiana Jones and the Kingdom of the Crystal Skull* to getting back on a bicycle. The composer has even said in some interviews that long-awaited additions to franchises are useful to revive the life of the original movies. It's certainly an easier scoring process for him than starting with nothing – and he would know, having returned to the galaxy far, far away twice after distinct hiatuses.

⸎

John Williams' office on the Universal Studios lot is a bungalow, steps away from Spielberg's production company. He will sit and work at his piano, preferring the instrument and a notepad and pencil to any digital composing software. 'I'm a great rewriter,' he explains. 'I scribble over things and change them. That's my own method. I started life as a pianist so I rely on the instrument more than most composers probably do.'

Spielberg tends to give Williams the book or script at the start of the project, but the composer is generally more keen to discuss the story with the director, to determine his outlook on the characters and narrative, and to watch footage of the film: 'I'd rather go into a projection room and react to the people and places and events – and particularly the rhythm – of the film itself.' After shooting the film, Spielberg will make a rough assembly of it to show Williams, and this first viewing is crucial for the composer to assess his initial response to the movie; he likens it to 'a doctor trying to diagnose somebody's physical condition'.

Spielberg has spoken of Williams' gift for 'spotting', knowing innately where to place music within a movie, and that the spotting sessions are, for him, one of the most enjoyable parts of the film-making process. They discuss whether a scene requires music, and if so, 'we talk about tempo, not so much in a harmonic or melodic context, but how fast or how slow the music should be. Tempo is the first thing a composer has to get right. The next thing has to do with how loud or how soft the music should be. Then, we determine the harmonic ambience and talk about emotions, texture.'

After the spotting sessions, Williams breaks down the scenes that need scoring onto a cue sheet and works on themes for characters or settings, and from there he'll tackle specific sequences. Here Williams is free to create, as Spielberg described in an interview in 1978: 'Once Johnny sits down at the piano, it's his movie, it's his score. It's his original overdraft, a super-imposition.'

While Williams works on the score, Spielberg will regularly pop round to his office, have a chat, and perhaps hear some themes played by John at the piano. Williams often has several themes in mind for a character, and Spielberg provides steers about which elements are most effective. Sometimes they will discuss combining the themes, or reassigning one to another character, but on other occasions a conversation might not even be necessary as the composer has said he can tell by Spielberg's reaction what he thinks about the music: 'I'll play two or three ideas for him in no particular order. Sometimes I have a favourite, sometimes I don't, but it's funny how you can always tell from people, from a glance, from their body language, how they feel about what they're hearing.' This intuitive approach, and the atmosphere of complete trust, makes their collaboration special, and the director is still clearly in awe of the composer's gift: 'I've always felt that John Williams was my musical rewrite artist. He comes in, sees my movie, rewrites the whole thing musically, and makes it much better than I did. He can take a moment and just uplift it.'

Now in his mid eighties, Williams has expressed shock in interviews when asked about retirement, stating that to him, composing is just as natural as breathing. He spends a couple of hours at the piano every day, and on the odd occasion when he doesn't have a pressing project, he continues to jot down ideas in his notebooks. His dedication to his art and to the process of composition is remarkable, as is his continued quest for the perfect music that will make the right connection between screen and audience.

⁓

One of the best examples of the extent to which Spielberg defers to his collaborator's musical vision is *E.T. the Extra-Terrestrial* (1982), a story of the friendship between a young boy and a creature from another planet. Spielberg has likened it to a sequel, of sorts, to *Close Encounters of the Third Kind*, and the music plays an important role, highlighting the bond between E.T. and Elliott. Williams compares the two: 'What makes them both successful is the fact that they affirm the fact that we are not alone in the universe. In the case of *Close Encounters*, the beginning of the film is much more terrifying because we don't know who these aliens are. But there is a great kind of uplifting feeling of almost religiosity, I think, at the end when we suddenly recognise that we have brothers and sisters. And so, there's a relief in the music. *E.T.* is also a bit scary in the beginning, but the minute we meet the little creature, the film becomes much more of a love story. That makes for a very different kind of musical challenge in *E.T.* as compared to *Close Encounters*.'

Steven Spielberg and John Williams during a rehearsal
for the score of *Saving Private Ryan*, 1998.

Williams composed an emotional score with a lyrical sense of wonder. The love theme feels tentative at first, but becomes more confident
within the film as the relationship between the boy and the alien grows,
building to fifteen minutes of continuous musical accompaniment in the
closing scenes, 'Escape/Chase/Saying Goodbye', and the story behind
the finale offers a remarkable insight into the working partnership
between the two: 'That sequence involved a lot of specific musical cues.
An accent for each speed bump of the bicycles; a very dramatic accent
for the police cars; a special lift for the bicycles taking off; sentimen-
tal music for the goodbye scene between E.T. and Elliott; and finally,
when the spaceship takes off, the orchestra swells up and hits an accent
as the spaceship whooshes away. So you can imagine in the space of that
fifteen minutes of film how many precise musical accents are needed

and how each one has to be exactly in the right place. I wrote the music mathematically to configure with each of those occurrences and worked it all out. Then when the orchestra assembled and I had the film in front of me, I made attempt after attempt to record the music to exactly all of those arithmetic parameters. But I was never able to get a perfect recording that felt right musically and emotionally. I kept trying over and over again and finally, I said to Steven, "I don't think I can get this right. Maybe I need to do something else." And he said, "Why don't you take the movie off? Don't look at it. Forget the movie and conduct the orchestra the way you would want to conduct it in a concert so that the performance is just completely uninhibited by any considerations of mathematics and measurement.'"

For a director to tell the composer to ignore his film and create music that felt right is practically unthinkable. Yet Spielberg had such faith in Williams' ability to enhance the emotional experience for the audience that he was happy to re-edit some parts to fit with the score as required. The result feels effortless, as the music places the audience at the heart of the action, from the bicycle chase and ride through the sky to Elliott's tearful farewell to his friend. It's hard to watch without being drawn in emotionally and the music plays a large part in that, swelling as the spaceship door closes, E.T. leaves and Elliott is left on earth.

꩜

The year 1993 was significant for Spielberg and Williams because they worked simultaneously on two projects and it would be hard to find two more different films. One, a harrowing historical drama about Oskar Schindler, a German businessman who saved over a thousand Jewish refugees from the Holocaust during the Second World War, and the other an adventure about a theme park inhabited by cloned dinosaurs. Both excellent in their own ways, but what a contrast.

Spielberg was editing *Jurassic Park* (1993) while shooting *Schindler's List* (1994). He was on location in Poland and would work three nights a week, via satellite, on post-production, having asked his good friend George Lucas to oversee some of the day-to-day technical tasks. He was also corresponding with Williams about the *Jurassic Park* music and the composer worked on both scores over a period of eight or nine months. The score for *Jurassic Park* is the more 'typically' Williams of the two, with a stirring, graceful theme to denote the dinosaurs and a secondary, brass-filled theme to underline the adventurous elements of the film. Director and self-confessed John Williams fan J.J. Abrams expressed his awe for the music: 'If you listen to the *Jurassic Park* theme, it begins with this incredible, very specific, memorable score, and you go, "Oh, of course, that's the *Jurassic Park* theme", but then it moves into the secondary piece and you go, "Oh no, *that's* the *Jurassic Park* theme", but they're both the *Jurassic Park* theme, so there's a level of incredible complexity but also emotion that he's somehow able to tap into. The fact that they co-exist is one of his remarkable gifts. Most composers, if they ever could even do one of those themes, would just do that one theme, and have a kind of secondary passage that would lead you back to that primary theme, but he is able to combine both.'

Despite the impact of the theme, it's worth noting that there is no music during the more dramatic set pieces, such as when the Tyrannosaurus rex attacks the children in the Jeep. What more do you need than dinosaur stomps and roars amid the lashing rain and screams of terror? Williams proves that a great film composer knows equally when not to score a scene as when music should be central to it.

In contrast with the *Jurassic Park* score, Williams' music for *Schindler's List* is an exercise in grief as well as hope. His aim for the main theme, which could easily be the slow movement of a violin concerto, was for it to be a lullaby of sorts, and it does provide an aching sort of comfort. Famously, the composer nearly did not score this film. He watched a screening of the whole movie, without music, and was so moved by it that he needed some fresh air before sitting down to discuss it with Spielberg. He went for a walk around the block to gather his thoughts and then told the director he needed a better composer for this film, to which Spielberg offered the now infamous comeback: 'I know, but they're all dead!' In the absence of Golden Age greats such as Max Steiner – often referred to as 'the father of film music' with scores for *Gone with the Wind* (1939) and *Casablanca* (1942) to his name – Williams was, in the director's opinion, the next best thing.

Both films amassed a total of ten Academy Awards in 1994, with *Jurassic Park* winning three technical awards and *Schindler's List* picking up seven, including the coveted Best Picture, Best Director and Best Original Score. That film marked a sea change in their respective careers, with Spielberg finally receiving recognition from the Academy for his work, which many critics had previously dismissed because of its blockbuster appeal. For the composer, the accolade – his fifth Oscar from fifty-one nominations – proved his power does not solely lie in rousing, brassy marches but also in understated emotion, and over the decades that followed he has stretched his skills between the two.

⁓

Spielberg won his second Best Director Oscar for ***Saving Private Ryan*** (1998); he recalls that 'restraint was John Williams' primary objective' in this film. There is only one hour of music for the film, which exceeds two hours, and there is no score for the long opening scene depicting the assault on Omaha Beach during the Normandy landings of 1944. The composer places music within the pauses that allow space for emotional reflection, such as the aftermath of the Omaha battle. The sparing use of music creates a richer whole, adding to the impact of the closing piece, 'Hymn to the Fallen', with its solemn brass and chorus, gradually fading out with a mournful military drum. The music serves as a memory: 'He did not want to sentimentalise or create emotion from what already existed in raw form. *Saving Private Ryan* is furious and relentless, as are all wars, but where there is music, it is exactly where John Williams intends for us the chance to breathe and remember'.

Williams' gift for restraint has added depth and dignity to war films and political dramas where a more showy score would feel smothering, such as his work with Oliver Stone, including *Born on the Fourth of July* (1989), and his later Spielberg projects, **Munich** (2005) and *War Horse*. He assesses the requirements of the film, working out whether, and how, the music will enhance our emotional connection to the story. For *Munich*, a thriller based on the aftermath of the Munich massacre at the 1972 Summer Olympics, in which the Israeli government sets out to find the Palestinian terrorists allegedly involved in the attack, the composer wanted to incorporate authentic sounds. He used the oud, a Middle Eastern lute, along with the cimbalom and a Hungarian zither. Steven Spielberg described the film as 'a prayer for peace' in that it set out to humanise both sides, and Williams' stand-out piece of that name provides a contemplation with sorrowful but understated strings that are imbued with hope.

Williams was inspired by the setting of the British countryside for **War Horse** (2011) and paints a bucolic picture with the opening flute of

'Dartmoor, 1912', followed by strings that are reminiscent of the music of Ralph Vaughan Williams. Unlike earlier collaborations with Spielberg in which one or two themes take centre stage, his music for this film offers a variety of motifs, taking the audience from pastoral peace to the trenches and back again, all the while reflecting the atmosphere of the period. The themes are woven throughout and tied together in the end credits suite, 'The Homecoming', in which the flute solo returns and Williams proves he really is the master of the orchestral score. Interestingly, Spielberg has described the music for *War Horse* as 'a stand-alone experience and it affected me deeply', indicating that it can take the audience on a journey without the film – surely not something most directors would care to admit.

✍

The Spielberg–Williams collaborations during the 2000s offer up yet wider variety of genres and styles. Some did not have the same impact on the box office or the critics as, say, *Jaws* or *Jurassic Park*, but the sheer range demonstrates a movie-maker and a musician who enjoy getting their teeth into new ways of storytelling.

The decade started back in science-fiction territory with ***A.I. Artificial Intelligence*** (2001) and *Minority Report*. Eyebrows were raised when it was announced that the typically 'happy-ever-after' Steven Spielberg was going to take over from the late, great Stanley Kubrick and direct a film about a robot who is programmed to love. Kubrick's intention may have been to create a more cold and clinical movie, whereas Spielberg and Williams explored the central question of the story: what it means to be human. The score can be divided into more atonal and minimalist sections, involving synthesisers and electric guitars, and a more 'human' angle, with a lullaby for soprano and orchestra. Kubrick, a master at selecting classical pieces for inclusion in his films, had planned to use *Der Rosenkavalier* by Richard Strauss, so Williams includes a quotation from it, all the while nodding to minimalist composers such as Philip Glass and Steve Reich.

For *Minority Report* (2002), a neo-noir film set in 2054 where people can be punished for crimes they have not yet committed, the composer and director wanted a score that was reminiscent of the Golden Age, like Adolph Deutsch's music for one of the first major film noirs, *The Maltese Falcon* (1941). This might seem counter-intuitive for a story based in the future, but Spielberg and Williams wanted to use the music to reflect the parts of the film that are based on memory and looking back to the past. The composer created a more adult-sounding, thrilling score, with hints of *Jaws* in its atmospheric foreboding, and shades of Bernard Herrmann, who he described as 'the grandparent of the score'.

There was further experimentation with earlier sounds in their twentieth collaboration, *Catch Me If You Can* (2002), which, with its 1960s setting, allowed Williams to revisit his jazz background. He composed a light and entertaining score that he described as a musical bonbon, and the saxophone and finger-snaps of the opening cue have a real swagger to them, instantly drawing the viewer into the film. The tune returns as the FBI gets ever closer to the conman Frank Abagnale, adding a sense of menace as the tension builds towards his arrest.

Williams returned again to jazzy styles with *The Adventures of Tintin: The Secret of the Unicorn* (2011), his first animation score – and Spielberg's first animated film, using motion-capture techniques, with Peter Jackson stretching his visual effects skills in the role of producer. Made in the same year as *War Horse*, the two projects were a refreshing contrast for the composer, as the heft of the war drama juxtaposed neatly with this send-up of early adventure films. Not dissimilar to *Raiders of the Lost Ark*, *Tintin* is reminiscent of Golden Age scores and the opening titles offer a charming homage to the era.

Williams composed various character themes, for Tintin, Captain Haddock, the Thompson twins and Snowy the faithful dog, and the result is a vibrant collection of music. As Spielberg comments, 'When I first heard the *Tintin* score, I felt as though John hadn't aged a bit since his work on *Jaws* and *Star Wars*. This new music has the same energy and exuberance, and it's so intricately interwoven into the story, characters, and images that it makes me feel like a youngster again.' There's a playfulness and joy in Williams' skills as a composer, and he would return to this light-hearted approach, with added childlike wonder, for their twenty-seventh collaboration, *The BFG* (2016).

There was yet another gear shift for ***Lincoln*** (2012), a notable project for Spielberg and Williams because it marked their fortieth anniversary of working together. It's a stately story of the final four months of America's sixteenth president as he sets out to ban slavery by ensuring that Congress passes the Thirteenth Amendment. At nearly three hours long, this is a sedate film, focusing on the political process. The score takes a back seat, filling roughly an hour, and the music allows the audience to reflect on what history can teach us. As Spielberg explains, 'John and I were here to guide and support this story, but not to make our voices heard above his.'

This is another occasion on which Williams exercises restraint, and in so doing reveals the emotional heart of the film. There is an intimacy to the orchestral performance, with fluid interplay between specific instruments, such as horn and piano, perhaps mirroring the individuals on-screen and their movements within the wider political landscape. The composer has said working on *Lincoln* was a very different experience compared with Spielberg films of the previous decade or so, and described it as a 'musical tapestry': as with his other war and political dramas, he has constructed pieces that capture hope amid the conflict. The result is a graceful, stirring and strangely personal score.

~

'I don't think there's been a single moment where we've had a disagreement about music,' stated Spielberg in 2012. 'We certainly have a high regard for each other, but I just think that's about Johnny hitting the target in an uncanny way.' Spielberg's nickname for Williams offers a touching insight into their friendship, highlighting the respect he has for Williams' music: 'I call him Max. As a matter of fact, when I named my first child Max, that came from a nickname that I gave Johnny from the first time we met. It's a joke that sometimes his music reminded me of Max Steiner. And he would always laugh, so I got to calling him Max.' Williams remains equally full of praise for Spielberg: 'Working with Steven has been a delight. He has the most wonderful personality and his goal is always to entertain people while also trying to improve the world.'

Williams certainly owes a debt to the 'father of film music' but over the decades he has built his own reputation as a movie master, revered by fans and aspiring composers alike for his stamp on the cinematic sound world. Spielberg has described him as 'one of the greatest storytellers of all time'. The truth is they both are, and that's where the key to their successful collaboration lies: their passion for film-making continues unabated from project to project, and they have always maintained a high regard for the story, and ensured that the audience is placed at the centre of it. From wartime heroes and friendly giants to aliens, dinosaurs and sharks, the Spielberg–Williams partnership has been welcomed into cinemas and households for generations, earning both director and composer a rightful place in film history.

 ## *Collaboration History*

*The Sugarland Express* (1974)

*Jaws* (1975)

*Close Encounters of the Third Kind* (1977)

*1941* (1979)

*Raiders of the Lost Ark* (1981)

*E.T. the Extra-Terrestrial* (1982)

*Indiana Jones and the Temple of Doom* (1984)

*Empire of the Sun* (1987)

*Always* (1989)

*Indiana Jones and the Last Crusade* (1989)

*Hook* (1991)

*Jurassic Park* (1993)

*Schindler's List* (1993)

*The Lost World: Jurassic Park* (1997)

*Amistad* (1997)

*Saving Private Ryan* (1998)

*A.I Artificial Intelligence* (2001)

*Minority Report* (2002)

*Catch Me If You Can* (2002)

*The Terminal* (2004)

*War of the Worlds* (2005)

*Munich* (2005)

*Memoirs of a Geisha* (2005), produced by Spielberg

*Indiana Jones and the Kingdom of the Crystal Skull* (2008)

*The Adventures of Tintin: The Secret of the Unicorn* (2011)

*War Horse* (2011)

*Lincoln* (2012)

*The BFG* (2016)

*The Post* (2017)

 ## Suggested Playlist

*The Sugarland Express*, Theme

*Jaws*, Title Theme

*Jaws*, The Shark Cage Fugue

*Close Encounters of the Third Kind*, End Titles

*1941*, March

*Raiders of the Lost Ark*, Raiders March

*Raiders of the Lost Ark*, Marion's Theme

*E.T. the Extra-Terrestrial*, Escape– Chase– Saying Goodbye

*E.T. the Extra-Terrestrial*, End Credits

*Empire of the Sun*, Exsultate Justi

*Empire of the Sun*, Cadillac of the Skies

*Indiana Jones and the Last Crusade*, Scherzo for Motorcycle and Orchestra

*Hook*, Flight to Neverland

*Jurassic Park*, Theme

*Schindler's List*, Remembrances

*Schindler's List*, Theme

*Amistad*, Dry Your Tears, Afrika

*Saving Private Ryan*, Hymn to the Fallen

*A.I Artificial Intelligence*, Where Dreams Are Born

*Catch Me If You Can*, Catch Me If You Can

*The Terminal*, Viktor's Tale

*Munich*, A Prayer for Peace

*The Adventures of Tintin: The Secret of the Unicorn*, Introducing the
  Thompsons, and Snowy's Chase

*War Horse*, Dartmoor, 1912

*War Horse*, The Homecoming

*Lincoln*, Freedom's Call

*Lincoln*, The People's House

*The BFG*, Dream Country

*The Post*, The Presses Roll

*The Post*, Mother and Daughter

# 12

# HANS ZIMMER AND CHRISTOPHER NOLAN

*'This is no time for caution.'*

Take one of the most successful and critically acclaimed film directors working today, add one of the most popular and versatile film composers, then sit back and prepare yourself for a thrilling collaboration. The partnership between Christopher Nolan and Hans Zimmer is a powerful one because they consistently demonstrate they are an equal match, each striving to experiment and push the boundaries of creativity.

Christopher Nolan is currently the sixth-highest-grossing director following the mighty top three of Steven Spielberg, Peter Jackson and James Cameron. At the time of writing, his films have received thirty-five Academy Award nominations and seven wins, with one of the hits of summer 2017, *Dunkirk*, in the running for eight categories at the Academy Awards in 2018. The British-American director, producer and screenwriter has mastered the art of balancing bankable movies with independent sensibilities and never assumes that blockbuster equals brainless. With only ten feature-length films under his belt, he has built such a strong reputation that audiences will flock to see something on the basis of it being a Christopher Nolan movie. Not many directors wield that power.

Hans Zimmer is also at the top of his game and has been for decades. The German composer has scored over 150 films and can turn his hand to animation just as easily as action, and to pretty much everything in between. An accomplished performer who packs out stadiums with his live shows, Zimmer won the Academy Award for Best Original Score for *The Lion King* in 1995 and has so far received ten other Oscar nominations for movies as varied as *Rain Man* (1988), *Sherlock Holmes* (2009), *The Thin Red Line* (1998) and *Gladiator* (2000). Despite a vast back catalogue, his scores are often described as having the 'Hans Zimmer sound', generally summarised by momentous crescendos and big, bold, electronic squelches that have been frequently copied, but when asked about his signature style, he drily knocks it back by pointing out a few other films he's worked on: *Driving Miss Daisy, As Good As It Gets, Frost/Nixon, Thelma and Louise* ... There is no one 'sound' when it comes to Hans Zimmer.

The director and composer first started working together in 2005 on *Batman Begins*, the first film in *The Dark Knight* trilogy that redefined the superhero movie genre. Fellow composer James Newton Howard collaborated with them on the first two films before ceding scoring duties wholly to Zimmer for the third, *The Dark Knight Rises*. Along with *Inception, Interstellar* and *Dunkirk*, Zimmer has scored six of Nolan's directorial features, cementing his role as Nolan's go-to composer. What's significant about their partnership is they genuinely collaborate on each project, to the extent that Zimmer has described Nolan as 'the co-creator of the score'. In the sleeve notes for *The Dark Knight*, the director notes, 'Hans sees through the screen to the dark beating heart of the story and is faithful to that and only that', and speaking in 2015 on the day his BAFTA nomination for *Interstellar* had been announced, Zimmer acknowledged his immersive approach: 'I think Chris wanted to work with me because of the way I work with directors, which is slightly different. I come in very early into the project, I get really in among it in the film-making process. I've got a big mouth, I keep asking questions, you know like "Why is the character doing this?" and "Do we need this shot?", and "Hang on, if you gave me that sort of a shot I could maybe do this, that and the other", and it takes a certain director who can embrace that.' Luckily, Nolan has.

~

Zimmer's career began as a performer, playing keyboards and synthesisers in bands including The Buggles, and his composing work took shape when he partnered up with Stanley Myers in the 1980s. Myers was a prolific film composer whose popular 'Cavatina', written originally for the movie *The Walking Stick* in 1970 and later used in *The Deer Hunter*, remains a Classic FM favourite, and he was something of a mentor to Zimmer. They collaborated on various films, including *My Beautiful Laundrette* (1985), although British audiences may be more familiar with his work on a TV show from this decade: Zimmer is the co-composer of the theme for *Going for Gold*.

Nolan aside, Zimmer has formed long-standing partnerships with other illustrious directors: seven films each with Ron Howard, including *Rush* (2013) and *The Da Vinci Code* (2006), and with Gore Verbinski, encompassing most of the *Pirates of the Caribbean* movies. His six films with Ridley Scott brought him acclaim, especially *Gladiator*, and his four collaborations with the late Tony Scott were also successful, not least *Crimson Tide* (2005), for which Zimmer received a Grammy Award. The composer is most often found at his Santa Monica studio, Remote Control Productions, which is quite the powerhouse for creating film and video-game scores, and Zimmer has collaborated with and mentored a host of composers there, including Ramin Djawadi (*Game of Thrones*), Harry Gregson-Williams (*The Martian*), Lorne Balfe (*The Lego Batman Movie*), John Powell (*How to Train Your Dragon*) and Rupert Gregson-Williams (*Wonder Woman*).

A largely self-taught musician, Zimmer doesn't compose on paper but writes using a computer, allowing him and the director to listen to a virtual score as a prototype. He describes how he sees his role: 'I never went to music school, my two weeks of piano lessons were two weeks wasted . . . I always write from a personal point of view and I love the directors that allow me to do that. I don't think there's a director that ever tells a composer what to do, not really, not a real director. It is your job to walk into the room and go, "I'm going to do something you can't even imagine." That's the job. And so you have to come in with a point of view and you have to come in with an idea, and it might be contrary to what the director is thinking of, but if it's a good idea, they'll embrace it.'

The absence of formal training may have made the composer more daring in his choices and approach, and in his ability to keep the music personal. He had never composed for animation before *The Lion King*, but for Zimmer the process developed into something he had not envisaged: 'Sometimes the best things happen for all the wrong reasons. I didn't want to do a cartoon but at the time I had a six-year-old daughter and I was desperate to show off and take my princess to the ball or premiere. I couldn't really take her to see one of Ridley's movies! So I said, "OK, I'll do it." I sat in front of these storyboards and I have no idea how

Christopher Nolan and Hans Zimmer attending a ceremony
for Zimmer's Hollywood Walk of Fame star, 2010.

to write about fuzzy animals. I'm listening to the story and it's the story
of a son losing his father at a really early age and that's what happened to
me in real life. I never dealt with it and suddenly I was confronted with
having to deal with the death of my father, and so it became really that.'

As with many of the directors featured in this book, Christopher Nolan
was fascinated by films from a young age, borrowing his father's Super 8
camera and making home movies. Speaking on the day of the *Dunkirk*
world premiere in London, he cited *Star Wars* and *2001: A Space Odyssey*
as two films that were formative musical influences, and also credited his
collaborator: 'I like to kid Hans because I'm a little bit younger than him,
but I started to come to his scores as a teenager, particularly for Ridley
Scott's *Black Rain*, which I think is a masterpiece of 1980s synthesiser

scores. In fact, one track from that really provided the seed of a lot that we did in *Batman Begins*, and expanded on and turned into something else. I would also point to Vangelis, particularly his work on *Bladerunner* and *Chariots of Fire* – those are fascinating scores in terms of the integration of synthesised elements with more classical harmonies, really interesting bridges between time periods.'

Nolan grew up between the UK and the USA. He read English Literature at University College London and was president of the film society. With some short films under his belt, his first feature, *Following*, was made in 1998, shortly after graduation. A self-funded project starring Nolan's friends and co-produced by Emma Thomas, now his wife and co-founder of his production company Syncopy, *Following* is a remarkable achievement. Shot over weekends in between the cast's and crew's full-time jobs, the neo-noir crime tale was well received, picking up awards at international film festivals and making the young director a name to watch.

Nolan's next film, **Memento** (2000), launched him into the big league, receiving two Academy Award nominations, for Best Editing and Best Original Screenplay. A puzzle of memory that plays with time and challenges the audience with plot twists and narrative devices, *Memento* was passed over for distribution by many big studios but became a real word-of-mouth hit. The structure is astonishingly assured, with two storylines – one told chronologically and the other told in reverse order – that meet at the end of the film. Nolan has described the writing process for his films in terms of geometric patterns, and he often draws diagrams when plotting his stories, which is unsurprising considering how so many of his projects avoid a linear narrative. *Memento* is so meticulously crafted that it is actually possible to watch the film backwards, scene by scene. Director Steven Soderbergh championed the film and the director, helping him to get his first big-budget thriller, the remake of the Norwegian film *Insomnia*, in 2002. Quite a leap from that self-funded debut when he'd used relatives' houses for film sets and his mum had helped out with the sandwiches between shoots.

Cheltenham-born composer David Julyan scored Nolan's first three features, having worked on his earlier shorts *Larceny* and *Doodlebug*, and they would collaborate again in 2006 for *The Prestige*, released between *Batman Begins* and *The Dark Knight*. Boasting another satisfying plot twist, this film was the first occasion on which the director utilised a specific and disorientating musical effect called the Shepard Tone, generated by the superimposition of sine waves separated by octaves: 'Done correctly, you create this illusion of a continuing rise in pitch that never goes out of range.' Nolan used it on the scores for *The Dark Knight* and *Dunkirk*, and also for sound effects: 'The Batpod, the motorbike version of the Batmobile that Batman drives in *The Dark Knight*, it never downshifts, so the engine continually rises in pitch – and that was based on experiments we'd done with Shepard Tones.' This description reveals much about Nolan's approach to film-making, with a focus on the small details of a production and an innate curiosity about the power of sound.

❧

Nolan had been working on a revival of the Batman story with screenwriter David S. Goyer since 2003. The caped crusader was last seen on the big screen in 1997 in the much derided *Batman and Robin*, and Nolan's and Goyer's vision was to tell the hero's backstory. No 'biffs!' and 'pows!' in this tale, which, with a noir sheen typical of the director, explains Bruce Wayne's fear of bats, how his parents died and why he chose to fight to defend Gotham City.

The *Dark Knight Trilogy* is still highly regarded by film-goers and directors, having influenced other comic-book movie franchises to explore darker tones and emotional depth, and the director knew he needed a confident pair of hands to score such a large-scale project weighted with expectation. In the sleeve notes for *The Dark Knight Rises*, Nolan explains he recruited Zimmer to help provide a 'fresh musical approach' for the reinvention of Batman, stating, 'For me, Hans Zimmer was the sound of contemporary movies.' The composer is said to have asked some difficult questions when they met to discuss the project, such as whether the music needed to sound 'heroic' in the first place, demonstrating 'an unerring ability to hone in on the one thought that cracks a project open'. For some time Zimmer had been wanting to work with his friend and fellow composer James Newton Howard, an eight-time Academy Award nominee perhaps best known for his long-standing collaboration with director M. Night Shyamalan, and suggested to Nolan that he bring him along for the ride.

Just as Zimmer may raise a few eyebrows by not composing with pen and paper, Nolan defies tradition by turning his back on temp scores, the standard way for a director to explain what he expects of the music. This technique, in which music is borrowed from other composers, may be in part responsible for the pervasive 'Hans Zimmer sound' aped by other composers, as they've been given Zimmer cues in temp scores and have wittingly or unwittingly imitated them to achieve the desired effect. As Zimmer explains, Nolan insists 'that no music shall ever be near the movie that wasn't written for the movie and in the past, for instance in the Batman movies, if I hadn't written a few reels they would just cut with no music'.

Another feature of Zimmer's and Nolan's collaborative world is that it includes other key members of the crew, notably the sound design and editing team. Lee Smith has been Nolan's editor since *Batman Begins* and Zimmer, who describes him as the director's 'number one', also has a long-standing rapport with him, the pair having first met over twenty years ago when Smith was director Peter Weir's sound editor: 'We all come from this sort of sonic world, and I think it's helpful. He can cut in silence because he can imagine it.' If Smith and Nolan reach a creative impasse, Zimmer can step in to offer a fresh perspective. On **Batman Begins** (2005), the director describes 'what I consider to be a great musical moment when the bats first surround Bruce Wayne, and we had a lot of trouble with a big wide shot at the end we were cutting to, trying to achieve the right grandeur. We kept putting it on the music and saying, "How do we do this, how do we hit it?" and Hans finally said, "Can you just have the bats fill the frame so it goes to black?" Lee and I looked at each other and thought, "Well, we missed that!" So we do that and magically Hans's music was already perfect.'

The piece in question is 'Barbastella', one of the stand-out moments from a decidedly un-heroic-sounding score. The cues are all named after different types of bat, and other musical highlights include 'Vespertilio', used during the flashback of the bats, and 'Eptesicus', which starts in a gentle manner then builds in strength as Bruce Wayne begins his training. The music is never overbearing but matches the action and emotion as and when required, and it's no surprise that Zimmer was immersed in the sound and editing as well as the scoring, or that Nolan would want him to become a regular part of the team. As the director puts it, 'That's the kind of creative collaboration you're looking for from the people you work with. I don't think it's possible for a composer to just be in their musical lane; I think you need somebody who's part of the team and more involved.' Many of the partnerships examined in this book have flourished because the composer stays within their creative realm while the director respects and acknowledges the importance of their music; it's interesting that Nolan actively encourages Zimmer to contribute to other parts of the film-making process.

Of course, Zimmer had the added benefit of collaborating with another composer on this score, and Newton Howard has previously explained that 'the combination of the two of us has become the voice of the score'. They worked on some themes separately, in offices across the hall from each other at the same studios where Nolan was working on post-production. Having two composers opened the scoring process up to a wider conversation, and the pair worked so closely they have said they can't remember which of them wrote specific cues in the film.

Following the critical and commercial success of *Batman Begins*, which received an Academy Award nomination for Best Cinematography and three BAFTA nods including Best Sound, the pressure was on for the second instalment in the trilogy, and it's safe to say Nolan raised the bar, and then some. The highest-grossing film of 2008, **The Dark Knight** is considered one of the finest superhero films ever made, and impressively for a film of this genre, it was nominated for eight Academy Awards, winning two, for Best Sound Editing and Best Supporting Actor, for Heath Ledger who played the Joker.

Once again, Zimmer threw himself into the score. He created 'The Joker Suite', around 10,000 bars of music that he has described as 'mayhem', which was his way of getting to the core of the villain's character and depicting his anarchy and fearlessness. Nolan apparently spent a long-distance plane journey dissecting around ten hours' worth of music and selecting the bars that he felt had impact, and this became a nine-minute piece, 'Why So Serious?' Throughout the film, the Joker's actions force characters to make difficult ethical decisions and the music reflects the escalating tension and chaos by employing the aforementioned

Shepard Tone along with near-deafening crescendos, such as in the mighty 'Aggressive Expansion', when swathes of strings, interspersed with pulsating rhythms, build to a crashing wall of sound.

Nolan was reportedly initially reticent to embark on a third film in the DC Comics universe, but together with his brother Jonathan and David S. Goyer, a story was devised that further explores the concept of heroism and expectations of a superhero film, as well as providing all the special effects required from a blockbuster action movie. Newton Howard was invited to return with Zimmer for the third film but declined, having seen how well Nolan and Zimmer gelled, not least with their work together on the interim film, *Inception*. For his part, Zimmer was keen to put his own stamp fully on the final instalment. He incorporated some of the earlier themes in **The Dark Knight Rises** (2012), such as the bat-flapping motif that accompanied the opening logo for all three films, but the inclusion of new characters allowed for the musical universe to be expanded. 'Gotham's Reckoning', the principal theme for villain Bane, is big, bold and portentous, whereas 'Mind If I Cut In?', Selina Kyle's theme, encompasses gentle piano with repetitive percussion and frantic strings, creating an intense aura of foreboding.

Again, Zimmer was hands-on with more than the score. Nolan acknowledges that 'there have been many things that have come from Hans, and not all of them musical, some of them really relating to story. He's an all-round creative collaborator.' One particular contribution was the scene at the start of a football match, just before the stadium is blown up by Bane. The director had been considering different options for this sequence and asked Zimmer to suggest well-known names who might want to appear singing 'The Star-Spangled Banner'. After throwing a few ideas into the ring, the composer called him to say the most fitting choice would be for a young boy to stand on the pitch singing the national anthem because this got right to the core of the story's emotional heart, and as Nolan acknowledges in the album sleeve notes, 'It was the sort of priceless contribution that gives you goosebumps and reveals your dangerous dependence on a collaborator.'

Zimmer is equally full of praise for Nolan's talents, and acknowledges that the director builds the environment in which the composer can participate and create – easier said than done in the world of big-budget films and major Hollywood studios: 'Here is the main thing that Chris does: he takes the terror away. He protects me. He surrounds me with a way to keep me safe.' Creating this place of safety and the two-way bond of trust involved in doing so is central to their collaborative success and strengthens their dynamic.

Zimmer describes the relaxed world they inhabit when working on a project together: 'Chris makes his movies in his garage – that's where his cutting room is – and my studio is very much set up like a living room . . . it's just two friends having a chat, and I'm near the keyboard and in the middle of the chat an idea will come. So there's a playfulness involved, and we are really rigorous at maintaining our privacy. People think Chris is very secretive but he's not secretive at all. To do what he does, you have to have the luxury of trying things out and some of these ideas might not work. You don't want to do that in front of the studio or the public, you want to do that within the family that is your core team.'

Having displayed his prowess at superhero scoring, Zimmer was the obvious choice when Nolan was working on a reboot of the Superman story. The score for *Man of Steel* (2013), co-written and co-produced by Nolan, works on a similarly broad palette, with sweeping action cues that are mini emotional journeys, such as 'Terraforming', and the brilliantly named 'What Are You Going to Do When You Are Not Saving the World?' Zimmer teamed up with fellow composer Tom Holkenborg (under his pseudonym Junkie XL) on the follow-up, *Batman v Superman: Dawn of Justice* (2016), of which Nolan was executive producer. Despite the poor-to-middling reviews for the film, the music fused orchestral and electronic sounds to powerful effect; if you are ever in need of a musical call to action, seek out 'Is She With You?'

⁓

In between *The Dark Knight* and *The Dark Knight Rises*, Nolan and Zimmer stepped away from Gotham City to collaborate on one of the most original films of the decade. A science-fiction heist film packed with intelligence, action and mind-bending special effects, *Inception* (2010) cemented Nolan's status as a writer and director with verve, vision and near-limitless imagination. He had submitted his idea of 'dream stealers' to Warner Bros. shortly after completing *Insomnia* but acknowledged such an ambitious project required more experience, so turned his attentions to *Batman Begins*. His original idea had more of a horror bent than the final dreams-within-dreams-within-dreams tale, which incorporated his trademark tropes of film noir and suspense, and on release *Inception* was many critics' film of the year, standing out as a one-off, complex blockbuster in a world often dominated by reboots, adaptations and sequels. *Inception* received eight Academy Award nominations, including one for Zimmer for Best Original Score, Best Original Screenplay (Nolan's second nod in that category) and the coveted Best Picture nomination, and it won four: Best Cinematography, Best Sound Mixing, Best Visual Effects and Best Sound Editing.

Encouraged by Nolan to try out new ideas (understandably, given the film is about stretching the boundaries of reality and perception),

Zimmer created an electronic score with an emotional heft. Driving rhythms and guitar give cues like 'Mombasa' a breathless urgency, and in the case of 'Time', waves of strings and glassy piano notes offer a moment of reflection before the sudden ending erupts into ambiguity. Most notable is the now ubiquitous *Braaam* sound that found fame in the trailers but was created by Zimmer in the opening track 'Half Remembered Dream'. Nolan had written Edith Piaf's song 'Je ne regrette rien' into the script and the aim was to introduce a different, slowed-down part of the song within each layer of dream in the film. Experimenting with that concept and aiming to create a sound of distant horns, Zimmer started with a piano in a church, put a book on the pedal and asked brass players to 'play into the resonance of the piano'. He added some electronic magic, and *Braaams* were born. They are now so commonplace in movie music that their origin is a bit of a touchy subject: composers Zack Hemsey and Mike Zarin were brought in to work on the music for the different *Inception* trailers, so some people place the credit with them, while others refer to trailers from earlier films, such as *District 9* (2009), to point out 'braaamsian' – if you will – qualities within them. For his part, Zimmer claims that he is the 'godfather of *braaams*', and that the inception of the famous, focused foghorn was born of Nolan's plan to use the Piaf song and Zimmer's subsequent experimentation to see what would happen if it was slowed down.

With *Inception*, Zimmer created impact and emotional connection through the layering of sounds, effects and music, and the digital manipulation thereof, as opposed to a 'typical' score – a technique he would later employ for *Interstellar*. The resulting soundscapes owe their success to neither director nor composer treating a film's music as a stand-alone entity: 'What I'm always interested in', Zimmer explains, 'is that we really try to create a whole sonic world.' As he points out, both *Inception* and

*Interstellar* deal with complex subjects and at times the audience may feel confused or lost within the intellectual framework of the story. Zimmer's belief is that the music should act like a river, moving the audience through the film: 'Like all journeys sometimes it might get a bit stormy, a bit rocky, but let's make sure if you enjoy the journey, there is something that guides you emotionally all the way through.'

❦

After dreams and superheroes, Nolan took us into space with *Interstellar* (2014). The tagline on the movie poster was 'Go Further' and that's clearly what the director set out to do. The story of a group of astronauts searching through a wormhole in the universe for a new home for humanity, when planet Earth becomes unsustainable, embraced vast themes and scientific possibilities, so it was even more crucial that the music got to the heart of the story. As Nolan describes it, 'When you're working with someone like Hans who is a great talent, a great genius . . . the challenge really is to challenge him . . . to find a way to destabilise him and destabilise his process, which he hates but he thanks you for it in the end!'

By this stage, composer and director had complete faith in each other, and both were keen to try out something different. 'One of the games we played,' said Zimmer, signalling that he and Nolan had fun as well as pushing each other creatively, 'because we felt what we had done for the Batman movies and what we had done for *Inception* had sort of seeped into the general film-music consciousness a little too much, was to go, "What are we not going to do?" Simple things like no string ostinatos, no action drummy things, there's none of that going on.'

Nolan was keen to get Zimmer involved as early as possible, due in part to his dislike of temp scores but primarily to allow him creative freedom that wasn't dictated by the narrative but, rather, fused within it. He set an unusual challenge, as the composer explains: 'He started off by coming to me and saying if he were to write one page but not tell me what the movie is about, would I give one day and write whatever came to mind? Of course I said yes, it sounds like fun, so he sent me this letter and inside it was this beautifully typewritten, rather thick piece of paper, [which] described the relationship between a father and his son. And a lot of the things which resonated in that with me were things that Chris knew very well about me and about my relationship with my children.' Zimmer spent a day writing and then called Nolan late on a Sunday evening to play him what he'd come up with. As Zimmer notes, 'It's always precarious when you play something to somebody for the first time', so he asked for Nolan's thoughts with trepidation: 'His answer was, "Well, I suppose I'd better make the movie now." To which what I said was "Well, what *is* the movie?"!'

As Nolan recalls, 'He didn't even know it was a science-fiction film. That was very important to me. So he wrote the piece of music that actually forms the basis for the entire score without even knowing the genre of the film, and that was a fascinating thing to do.' Zimmer was initially confused about the scale of the story and the deceptively simple piano tune he'd written, 'Day One': 'At one point I said to him, "Hang on a second, I've just written you the most intimate, tiny, personal theme, really, about my son", and he said, "Yes, but I now know where the heart of the movie is", and in a funny way that became an important cornerstone for the score.' Nolan listened to 'Day One' as he worked on the script, so music influenced content, just as he'd desired. Somehow, it's fitting for a story that takes the audience over space and time that the music and story are so intimately entwined, and the composer described the process of creation – with script and score determining each other – as 'two musicians jamming together. We know the song we sort of want to play and then we go and improvise on that.'

The score sounds a universe away from the Zimmer *Braaams* and is elevated by the ethereal power of the pipe organ. The director suggested using the instrument before the composer had written anything apart from the initial piano piece because 'it always seemed to me that he should have written an organ score and he hadn't until that point. In talking to him it became apparent that [he] had a huge connection emotionally with the pipe organ, but hadn't really used it in scores other than in small ways.' A young Hans used to play a 2,500-pipe baroque organ belonging to a family friend, an elderly organist whom he credits as influencing his choice of career path, and as well as having such a personal connection to the instrument, he explains that the very structure of the organ, and its role in history, resonated with a film about scientific and technological breakthroughs: 'By the seventeenth century the church organ was the most complex human creation, and it maintained that pivotal position of complexity until the telephone exchange was invented, and one of the things that was really important to us as a subtext for the movie was to celebrate human endeavour.'

Of course it's not just what the organ represents but its sound – and what a sound! Nolan hadn't initially appreciated the magnitude of using such an intricate instrument: 'What I didn't know because I'm not a musician is how unbelievably difficult and cumbersome it is to write to and work with ... It required a radically different approach from him and it was amazing to watch Hans rise to that challenge.' Zimmer completed the score on his computer, gleefully experimenting with the sounds from thousands of individual pipes from the organ in Salisbury Cathedral, which had been painstakingly recorded by sound engineer Brett Milan, whose software recreates digital equivalents of existing organs such as the 1877

Henry Willis instrument at Salisbury. Zimmer's organ works were dubbed onto the final film, and many crew members thought the score was done and dusted, but then the composer and director decided to go to the UK to see whether a church acoustic could enhance the electronic score.

Zimmer admits in the *Interstellar* sleeve notes that he was nervous about the recording sessions at the Temple Church in London because his music had not been limited by the practicalities of playing an organ – 'I never censored my imagination by wondering if it was even humanly possible to play' – and he voiced his concerns to Nolan. The pair agreed to temper their ambitions, deciding that if they returned with only one interesting sound or experiment, it would still have been worth it. But as Zimmer later revealed, he needn't have worried, thanks to the talented organist Roger Sayer: 'In the best English understatement, after Roger looked at the parts, he said, "Maybe I should go and try some of this", and he was absolutely extraordinary. From the first note we knew it was going to work.'

The woodwind and brass sections were recorded in a former church, AIR Studios, and the musicians were tested with directions such as 'Can we make the sound of wind howling through a cornfield?' – in keeping with the experimental process. It is a glorious score, featuring the rippling and haunting 'Dust' and atmospheric 'Stay', which starts quietly before the organ swells, incorporating magnificent layering from the strings before an unexpected finish. The composer plays the piano parts, staying faithful to the core of the project, and his Academy Award nomination for Best Original Score – one of the five nominations *Interstellar* received – was richly deserved.

Zimmer has said that throughout his career, he has a tendency to finish scoring with a sense that he could have done or given more, and the first time he didn't feel that was on *Interstellar*. During post-production, he and Nolan watched the whole film every Friday and made adjustments to the score, and one Friday, shortly before they were due to finish, he was able to tell the director he had no further changes to make. He had had enough time.

At the end of filming, Nolan gave Zimmer a watch inscribed with a line from the film that the composer cites as their working motto: 'This is no time for caution.'

～

The director gave the composer another watch for their next project, based on the true story of Operation Dynamo, which rescued hundreds of thousands of British soldiers from the beach of Dunkirk in 1940. This time, however, it was intended to feature in the score: 'I had made some recordings of different watches that I have, and I chose one recording that I'd made of a pocket watch that I own that has a particularly insistent ticking.'

*Dunkirk* (2017) is a remarkable triptych told from land, sea and air, written by Nolan according to a structure similar to the Shepard Tone, with the three elements being braided together in different ways to build the intensity. It is less a typical war film and more an exercise in suspense, as the audience is dropped into the heart of the action, provided with no backstory to the characters or external scenes featuring the enemy or the soldiers' lives and families back in Blighty – put simply, it's about getting home. Sound plays a vital role, and required a wider collaboration with the sound design and editing team, a working environment Zimmer has proved he thrives in. Nolan recruited the composer early on in the process and showed him the succinct script – at around seventy-six pages, it was about half as long as his others. That was deliberate, Nolan explains: 'We're trying not to tell the story through words; we're trying to create

235

suspense with image, sound and music. In the editing, we were layering in the sound effects and these tracks according to this rhythm, as we were cutting picture, so in that way, for better or for worse, we've been able to achieve a fusion of music, effects and picture in *Dunkirk* that we've never really been able to achieve before.' Watching *Dunkirk* is a truly visceral experience. It's not possible to separate sound from vision; it feels like film-making and storytelling at its purest. It's no surprise that three of *Dunkirk*'s eight Oscar nominations are for sound: Best Sound Mixing, Best Sound Editing and Best Original Score.

The composer spent months building tracks from the ticking of the director's pocket watch, and started integrating sirens and alarms that would build tension and 'instil a fear or panic' in the audience. Despite enthusiasm from Nolan, the process became increasingly difficult for Zimmer because, as the director explained, 'There's a coming together of things over a long period of time that did not involve tune, did not involve emotion, and I think that's a very difficult and frustrating position for a composer to be in. This was a very hard-fought score, there's no question.' Zimmer was instructed to hold back, to enhance the suspense objectively. Nolan was clear throughout that he did not want any emotion in the music 'because *Dunkirk* is freighted with emotion', which as he freely acknowledged was frustrating for a composer and musician who had trained himself to strive relentlessly to find the musical and emotional heart of a film. The resulting tracks like 'Supermarine' and 'The Oil' are claustrophobic and perfectly pitched.

The emotion builds within the score as the film progresses, heightened by the inclusion of 'Nimrod' from the *Enigma Variations* by Edward Elgar. It was a bold decision to incorporate such a familiar piece, and Nolan was very keen that it be embedded within the score, instead of feeling tacked on: 'One of the things I really don't like in film scores is when there's a commitment to an original score that's then, towards the end, up-ended or violated by the inclusion of a pre-existing piece of music.' Zimmer and another composer, Benjamin Wallfisch, threaded themes from *Nimrod* within the score, often heavily disguised or reworked, hinting at what's to come, so that when the piece becomes more evident in 'Variation 15 (Dunkirk)', it feels authentically organic to the film. As Nolan puts it, 'The emotion at the end of the film has to feel earned, narratively and musically.'

❧

Nolan and Zimmer work so well together because they think big. The director sets the bar high, and both then strive to surpass it. Their mutual respect is evident, for each other, the cast and crew, and, most crucially, the audience. As Zimmer says, 'Chris and I, everybody on Chris's team, work so hard at making the cinema sound good because it's such a compliment and an honour that somebody spent their hard-earned cash to come and have an experience.'

The pair clearly enjoy spending time in each other's company as well as the chance to rise to the challenge each new film provides. 'I don't think either of us is interested in repeating what we've done before, or having things be easy,' says Nolan. 'You hope to have fun, but you do want to challenge yourself. We tend to approach every film as trying to – and it sounds ridiculous to say out loud – to reinvent music or the musical language.' It's not just about vast ambitions though: Zimmer appreciates how Nolan has created the best working environment for him. 'At the end of the day – and Chris does it probably better than anybody else – the main job the director has with the composer is to cheer you on, to make sure you succeed, because if you succeed it helps the film to succeed.' Nolan disputes this 'very rose-tinted picture': 'We fight like cats and dogs but in the best, the most productive way. We love each other, with everything that comes with that. We fight like brothers at times and we love like brothers. It's an extraordinary partnership and a wonderful creative collaboration, but we dive into things fully, and when you do that, passions run high.'

 ## *Collaboration History*

All produced, written (or co-written) and directed by Christopher Nolan unless otherwise stated.

*Batman Begins* (2005), co-composed with James Newton Howard

*The Dark Knight* (2008), co-composed with James Newton Howard

*Inception* (2010)

*The Dark Knight Rises* (2012)

*Man of Steel* (2013), produced by Christopher Nolan

*Interstellar* (2014)

*Batman v Superman: Dawn of Justice* (2016), executive produced by Christopher Nolan; co-composed with Junkie XL

*Dunkirk* (2017)

 ## *Suggested Playlist*

*Batman Begins*, Vespertilio

*Batman Begins*, Eptesicus

*The Dark Knight*, Aggressive Expansion

*The Dark Knight*, Why So Serious?

*Inception*, Time

*Inception*, Mombasa

*Inception*, Dream is Collapsing

*The Dark Knight Rises*, Gotham's Reckoning

*The Dark Knight Rises*, Mind If I Cut In?

*The Dark Knight Rises*, The Fire Rises

*Interstellar*, Day One

*Interstellar*, Dust

*Interstellar*, S.T.A.Y

*Interstellar*, Stay

*Interstellar*, Rise

*Dunkirk*, Supermarine

*Dunkirk*, The Oil

*Dunkirk*, Variation 15 (Dunkirk)

*Dunkirk*, End Titles (Dunkirk)

# NOTES

All quoted material taken from interviews with Classic FM unless otherwise noted.

## 1: Carter Burwell and the Coen Brothers

Page 9, 'improvised using . . . peanut butter jars, etc.'
www.carterburwell.com/projects/Raising_Arizona.html.

Page 9, 'No one other than . . . orchestral music!'
www.carterburwell.com/projects/Millers_Crossing.shtml.

Page 10, 'a shimmering . . . notes'
www.carterburwell.com/projects/Fargo.shtml.

## 2: Patrick Doyle and Kenneth Branagh

Page 25, 'The only device . . . and then joined.'
Patrick Doyle interviewed by Philippe Blumenthal for *Soundtrack! The Collector's Quarterly*, vol. 16 no. 62 (June 1997).

Page 25, 'Apart from . . . modern instruments.'
ibid.

## 3: Danny Elfman and Tim Burton

Page 36, 'It is as important . . . in the films.'
Tim Burton interviewed in 1991 for David Breskin, *Inner Views: Filmmakers in Conversation* (Faber and Faber, London, 1992); reprinted in Kristian Fraga (ed.), *Tim Burton Interviews* (University Press of Mississippi, Jackson MS, 2005), p. 61.

Page 36, 'It's trying to show . . . kind of stuff.'"
Tim Burton in conversation with Danny Elfman for *Interview* magazine in 2010:
www.interviewmagazine.com/film/tim-burton/#page2.

Page 37, 'Writing the score . . . half-psychiatrist.'
Danny Elfman, interviewed for the *Guardian* in 2013:
https://www.theguardian.com/film/2013/oct/02/danny-elfman-tim-burton-singing.

Page 38, '[Price] was so great . . . with you forever.'
*Interview* magazine.

Page 38, 'I knew who Pee-wee . . . that simple.'
Danny Elfman interviewed for *Rolling Stone* in 2015: www.rollingstone.com/movies/ news/danny-elfman-on-film-scores-simpsons-and-working-with-tim-burton-20150629.

Page 39, 'I always thought . . . responded to your work.'
*Interview* magazine.

Page 39, 'Hearing the music . . . like that.'
Mark Salisbury (ed.), *Burton on Burton*, rev. edn (Faber and Faber, London, 2000), p. 48.

Page 41, 'There was a weird incident . . . the screening.'
ibid., p. 66.

Page 42, 'I don't think . . . into the film.'
ibid., p. 81.

Page 43, 'Danny and I . . . similar that way.'
Fraga, *Tim Burton Interviews*, p. 61.

Page 46, 'We'd worked together . . . pass on them.'
Salisbury, *Burton on Burton*, p. 121.

Page 47, 'I was the singer . . . They're your songs."'
Danny Elfman interviewed for *Vulture* in 2015: www.vulture.com/2015/07/danny-elfman-on-8-of-his-iconic-scores.html.

Page 47, 'I think he was mad . . . a bunch of kids, fighting'
Salisbury, *Burton on Burton*, p. 153.

Page 47, 'We're taking a little vacation from each other.'
ibid., p. 142.

Page 48, 'I think . . . working with Howard.'
ibid., p. 153.

Page 53, 'The music is . . . the context.'
Fraga, p. 61.

### 4: Michael Giacchino and J.J. Abrams

Page 58, 'a window . . . the piece'
From '*Mission Impossible III A Strike of a Match*', a 2006 interview by Randy Koppl for *Music from the Movies* magazine, no. 50, p. 54.

Page 60, 'It's a weird thing . . . hit the ground running.'
ibid., p. 55.

Page 61, 'It got to a place . . . shouldn't be.'
ibid.

Page 65, 'For some reason . . . push each other.'
ibid.

Page 65, 'I start to play . . . I can find things.'
ibid., p. 56.

Page 65, 'was informing . . . around'
ibid.

Page 71, 'If you . . . feel the story.'
ibid., p. 54.

Page 72, 'There is . . . effortlessness to it.'
ibid., p. 55.


## 5: Bernard Herrmann and Alfred Hitchcock

Quotations from interviews with François Truffaut are taken from François Truffaut, *Hitchcock* (Simon and Schuster, New York, 1967).

Page 79, 'purest form of cinema'
ibid.

Page 82, 'the work of a talented amateur'
ibid.


## 7: Maurice Jarre and David Lean

Page 120, 'terrible'
Gene D. Phillips, *Beyond the Epic: The Life and Films of David Lean* (University Press of Kentucky, Lexington KY, 2006), p. 304.

Page 121, 'something left over from *The King and I*'
ibid., p. 305.

Page 121, 'Sam, what is all . . . the nonsense!'
ibid.

Page 121, 'Sam, this chap . . . to do it!'
ibid.

Page 125, 'I think a composer . . . it should do.'
Gerald Pratley, *The Cinema of David Lean* (A. S. Barnes and Company, South Brunswick and New York, 1974), p. 187.

Page 128, 'He will write . . . where the music's going.'
David Lean, interviewed by Joseph Gelmis, 1970, in Steven Organ (ed.), *David Lean: Interviews* (University Press of Mississippi, Jackson MS, 2009), p. 41.

Page 128, 'There are anything . . . hard to describe.'
ibid.

Page 129, 'I get a tremendous . . . immensely exciting.'
Interview with Melvyn Bragg in 1985 for a *South Bank Show* special: *David Lean: A Life in Film*.

Page 130, 'I always participate . . . fix those lapses.'
'David Lean: The Legend of the Century', interview with Michel Spector, *Studio* magazine, 1989; in Organ (ed.), *David Lean: Interviews*.

Page 131, 'very demanding'
Phillips, *Beyond the Epic*, p. 427.

Page 132, 'David Lean once . . . the terminally ill!'
Interview with James Fitzpatrick from the sleeve notes for *Film Music Masterworks – Maurice Jarre* (Silva Screen Records, 2007).

Page 132, 'a master of . . . service of cinema'
*A Passage to India*, DVD extra (Acorn Media, 2012).

Page 133, 'I owe him everything . . . a great friend.'
https://www.theguardian.com/film/2009/mar/30/maurice-jarre-dies

### 9: Howard Shore and Peter Jackson
Page 154, 'just in terms . . . been gruelling.'
Paul A. Wood (ed.), *Peter Jackson: From Gore to Mordor* (Plexus Publishing, Ultra Screen series, London, 2005), p. 123.

Page 154, 'There was no room . . . for so long.'
ibid., p. 124.

Page 157, 'Howard's music . . . conversation with Howard.'
Peter Jackson interviewed by Rudy Koppl, *Music from the Movies*, 42 (2004), p. 19.

Page 157, 'who would be . . . of the team'
ibid.

Page 158, 'Howard was . . . seems to work.'
ibid., p. 20.

Page 159, '*The Lord of the Rings* . . . to Middle-earth.'
ibid., p. 19.

Page 162, 'One of the things . . . the scoring stage.'
ibid., p. 21.

Page 164, 'part of the job is supporting the composer'
ibid., p. 29.

Page 164, 'He said, "I'd like . . . made sense to Howard.'
ibid.

Page 165, 'the most important music of all three films'
ibid., p. 82.

Page 166, 'couldn't have actually . . . gratitude for him doing that.'
ibid.

Page 169, 'total control of every aspect'
Ian Pryor, *Peter Jackson: From Prince of Splatter to Lord of the Rings* (Random House, Auckland, New Zealand, 2003), p. 310.

Page 169, 'the last word'
ibid., p. 306.

Page 171, 'not just a book, but a whole mythic philosophy'
Paul A. Wood, *Peter Jackson*, p. 10.

Page 171, 'completely changed the way I work'
Rudy Koppl, *Music from the Movies*, p. 65.

Page 172, 'I've also learned a lot about patience, he's one of the most patient people I've ever met.'
ibid., p. 82.

Page 172, 'It's a wonderful . . . Fran and I have.'
ibid.

## 10: Alan Silvestri and Robert Zemeckis
Page 177, 'I was fascinated . . . technical end first.'
Interview with Robert Zemeckis in Robert J. Emery, *The Directors – Take Two: In Their Own Words* (TV Books, 2000), p. 66.

Page 178, 'a good guy . . . a solid human being'
Interview with Robert Zemeckis by Rudy Koppl in 2000, *Soundtrack*, vol. 19 no. 75: www.runmovies.eu/alan-silvestri-on-scoring-what-lies-beneath/

Page 182, 'Every movie . . . good trend or not.'
Robert J. Emery, *The Directors Cut*, p. 78.

Page 182, 'I was able ... willing to work.'
ibid., p. 82.

Page 184, 'That is like gold ... objectivity any more.'
Jeremy Kagan (ed. and moderator), *Directors Close Up: Interviews with Directors Nominated for Best Film by the Directors Guild of America*, 2nd edn (Scarecrow Press, Lanham MD, 2006), p. 254.

Page 185, 'I just hope ... familiar territory'
Robert J. Emery, *The Directors Cut*, p. 85.

Page 186, 'You develop ... the look on my face.'
www.runmovies.eu/alan-silvestri-on-scoring-what-lies-beneath/

Page 188, 'What he taught me ... and change it.'
ibid.

Page 189, 'creative soulmate'
ibid.

Page 189, 'He doesn't just ... a movie here.'
ibid.

## 11: John Williams and Steven Spielberg

Page 193, 'John has transformed ... made together'
Sleeve notes from *The Spielberg/Williams Collaboration* (Sony Classical, 1990).

Page 194, 'the only person that I've had a perfect association with'
Susan Royal, 'Steven Spielberg in His Adventures on Earth', *American Premiere*, July 1982, pp. 84–107; reprinted in Lester D. Friedman and Brent Notbohm (eds), *Steven Spielberg: Interviews* (University Press of Mississippi, Jackson MS, 2000), p. 92.

Page 194, 'The best directors ... a musical art.'
Irwin Bazelon, *Knowing the Score: Notes on Film Music* (Van Nostrand Reinhold, New York, 1975), p. 199.

Page 196, 'because I found the score so inspirational'
*Jaws*, 25th Anniversary Collector's Edition soundtrack, sleeve notes (Decca, 2000).

Page 197, 'To this day ... the film.'
Steven Spielberg interviewed by Laurent Bouzereau, *Jaws* soundtrack sleeve notes.

Page 197, 'At first I began to laugh ... the entire score.'
ibid.

Page 198, 'Suddenly, ... dramatic outline.'
John Williams interviewed by Laurent Bouzereau, *Jaws* soundtrack sleeve notes.

Page 198, 'even before . . . about *Close Encounters*'
Mitch Tuchman, 'Close Encounter with Steven Spielberg', *Film Comment*, 1978, p. 51;
Lester D. Friedman and Brent Notbohm (eds), *Steven Spielberg: Interviews*.

Page 199, '*Close Encounters* is . . . than *Star Wars.*'
Derek Ellis, 'The Film Composer: John Williams', *Films and Filming*, vol. 24 no. 10 (July 1978), p. 22.

Page 200, They kept returning to one particular sequence . . .
ibid., pp. 22–3.

Page 202, I'm a great rewriter . . . probably do.'
ibid., p. 24.

Page 202, 'I'd rather go . . . the film itself.'
ibid., p. 23.

Page 202, 'a doctor trying to diagnose somebody's physical condition'
Interview with John Williams, *E.T. the Extra-Terrestrial* 20th Anniversary Edition soundtrack sleeve notes (MCA/Universal Studios, 2002).

Page 203, 'we talk about tempo . . . emotions, texture.'
ibid.

Page 203, 'Once Johnny sits . . . a super-imposition.'
Mitch Tuchman, 'Close Encounter with Steven Spielberg'.

Page 203, 'I'll play two . . . they're hearing.'
Interview with John Williams, *E.T. the Extra-Terrestrial* 20th Anniversary Edition soundtrack sleeve notes.

Page 203, 'I've always felt . . . just uplift it.'
ibid.

Page 204, 'What makes them . . . as compared to *Close Encounters.*'
ibid.

Page 205, 'That sequence involved . . . mathematics and measurement.'"
ibid.

Page 208, 'restraint was John Williams' primary objective'
Interview with Steven Spielberg, *Saving Private Ryan* soundtrack sleeve notes (DreamWorks Records, 2000).

Page 209, 'He did not want . . . breathe and remember'
ibid.

Page 210, 'a stand-alone experience and it affected me deeply'
Commentary by Steven Spielberg from the *War Horse* film soundtrack sleeve notes (DreamWorks Records, 2011).

Page 211, 'the grandparent of the score'
Emilio Audissino, *John Williams's Film Music: Jaws, Star Wars, Raiders of the Lost Ark, and the Return of the Classical Hollywood Music Style* (University of Wisconsin Press, Madison WI, 2014), p. 218.

Page 212, 'When I first heard . . . a youngster again.'
Commentary by Steven Spielberg from *The Adventures of Tintin: The Secret of the Unicorn* soundtrack sleeve notes (Sony Music, 2011).

Page 213, 'musical tapestry'
emanuellevy.com/comment/lincoln-john-williams-music/

Page 213, 'I don't think . . . an uncanny way.'
John Burlingame, 'Spielberg and Lucas on Williams: Directors Reminisce about Collaborating with Hollywood's Greatest Composer', interview for the Film Music Society, February 2012: http://www.filmmusicsociety.org/news_events/features/2012/020812.html

Page 213, 'I call him Max . . . calling him Max.'
ibid.

Page 213, 'Working with Steven . . . improve the world.'
Interview with John Williams, *Jaws* 25th Anniversary Collector's Edition soundtrack sleeve notes.

## 12: Hans Zimmer and Christopher Nolan

Page 226, 'the combination of the two of us has become the voice of the score'
Interview with Hans Zimmer and James Newton Howard, 2009, KCRW; transcript, kcrw.com.

Page 230, 'play into the resonance of the piano'
www.indiewire.com/2013/11/hans-zimmer-feels-horrible-when-his-inception-bramms-are-used-in-movie-trailers-92087/

# ABOUT CLASSIC FM

Classic FM is the UK's biggest single commercial radio station and the most popular classical music brand, reaching 5.4 million listeners every week. Classic FM's programmes are hosted by a mix of classical music experts and household names including John Suchet, Alexander Armstrong, Myleene Klass, Bill Turnbull, Alan Titchmarsh, Charlotte Hawkins, Aled Jones, Margherita Taylor and Nicholas Owen. Since its launch in 1992, Classic FM has aimed to make classical music accessible and relevant to everyone and in doing so, introduce an entirely new audience to the genre. ClassicFM.com is the UK's biggest classical music website and has 1.7 million unique monthly web and app users. Classic FM is owned by Global. It is available across the UK on 100-102 FM, on DAB digital radio and TV, at ClassicFM.com and on the Classic FM app.

Source: *RAJAR/Ipsos-MORI/RSMB, period ending 17 September 2017.*

# ACKNOWLEDGEMENTS

Huge thanks, first and foremost, to all of the directors and composers featured here. I am particularly grateful to those who took the time to speak to me specifically for this book: Carter Burwell, Patrick Doyle, Sam Mendes, Howard Shore and Alan Silvestri. Thanks also to Sara Horner and Howard Goodall for their contributions, to NPR journalist Tim Greiving, and to Charlotte Green, Anne-Marie Minhall and Tommy Pearson, whose archive Classic FM interviews are cited here. I am very grateful to the staff and research resources at the BFI Reuben library, to Caeshia St Paul in the Global Enterprises team, to Olivia, Pippa, Jennie and Lorne at Elliott & Thompson, and to Sam Jackson and the entire Classic FM programming family.

A special thanks goes to Andrew Collins, not just for being a joy to work with on *Saturday Night at the Movies* and for the use of his archive Classic FM interviews, but for his advice throughout the research and writing process.

Finally, my thanks to the *Saturday Night at the Movies* listeners for sharing our passion for film scores – and to you for reading this book.

# INDEX